DK EYEWITNESS TRAVEL

TOP 10
MILAN
& THE LAKES

REID BRAMBLETT

Penguin
Random
House

Top 10 Milan and the Lakes Highlights

The Top 10 of Everything

CONTENTS

Milan and the Lakes Area by Area

Streetsmart

Within each Top 10 list in this book, no hierarchy of quality or popularity is implied. All 10 are, in the editor's opinion, of roughly equal merit.

Front cover and spine *Varenna, Lake Como*
Back cover *The Duomo Cathedral of Milan*
Title page *Galleria Vittorio Emmanuele II in central Milan, Italy*

Welcome to
Milan & the Lakes

Fast-moving and vibrant, Milan is the capital of Italy's north, and a world leader in the fields of fashion and design. Yet, behind the city's frenetic public face, there's another Milan with a rich cultural heritage, while just beyond its borders lie the tranquil jewels of the Italian lakes. With Eyewitness Top 10 Milan and the Lakes, it's all yours to explore.

World-class museums and stunning architecture; top restaurants and traditional trattorias; chic boutiques and bustling markets; grand opera and hot night spots – Milan has it all. And whether you are gazing in awe at **Leonardo's Last Supper** or looking out across the city from the roof of the **Duomo**, Milan is a sightseeing paradise. As befits a city with fashion at its heart, no mere shopping mall can compete with the grand and glorious **Galleria Vittorio Emanuele II**, while, for culture vultures, the **Pinacotera di Brera, Pinacoteca Ambrosiana** and the museums of **Castello Sforzesco** offer an unequalled guided tour through the entire history of Western art.

The Italian lakes are just a stone's throw away and make an idyllic contrast to busy Milan. Elegant **Lake Como** and **Lake Maggiore**, with their majestic villas and elaborate gardens, are the nearest, while laid-back **Lake Iseo** and beautiful **Lake Garda** are easily reached as well. The historic and cultural gems of **Bergamo** and **Mantua** are also close enough to merit a day's exploration.

Whether you're coming for a weekend or a week, our Top 10 guide brings together the best of everything the city and beyond can offer, from futuristic **Porta Nuova** to arty **Brera**, from the **Navigli** district's urban waterways to the **Isole Borromee**. The guide gives you tips throughout – from seeking out what's free to avoiding the crowds – as well as nine easy-to-follow itineraries designed to help you visit a clutch of sights in a short space of time. Add inspiring photography and detailed maps, and you've got the essential pocket-sized travel companion. **Enjoy the book, and enjoy Milan and the Lakes.**

Clockwise from top: Galleria Vittorio Emanuele II in Milan, spires of Milan's Duomo, Palazzo Te in Mantua, Varenna, Rocca di Angera frescoes, Triennale Design Museum, Lake Garda

Exploring Milan and the Lakes

Milan's city districts are many and varied, and each has its own well-defined character; moving from one to another can be a kaleidoscopic experience. The city's main monuments, galleries and shopping areas are relatively close together, however, within the compact and walkable historic centre.

Milan's **Duomo** affords magnificent city views from its Gothic-spired rooftop.

Two Days in Milan

Day ❶

MORNING

Start the day at Piazza Duomo to marvel at the Gothic **Duomo** (see pp14–15) and ascend to the roof for views as far as the Alps. Then it's just a hop to the **Quadrilatero d'Oro** (see p71) for window-shopping among the temples of fashion and coffee at historic **Cova** (see p88).

AFTERNOON

Cross Piazza Duomo to browse the **Galleria Vittorio Emanuele II** (see p75) and stamp on the "lucky bull".

Galleria Vittorio Emanuele II is Milan's unique, spectacular shopping arcade.

Spend the rest of the day in the **Pinacoteca di Brera** (see pp16–19) before dinner at **Latteria** (see p97).

Day ❷

MORNING

Castello Sforzesco (see pp20–21) is your first destination, followed by a stroll through **Parco Sempione** (see p92). From here walk along stylish Corso Como to the futuristic **Piazza Gae Aulenti** (see p94) and visit the bohemian Isola district just beyond. Have lunch at **Ratanà** (see p97).

AFTERNOON

Head to **Navigli** (see pp28–9) for a boat trip and an evening enjoying the canalside bars for happy hour and then dinner at **El Brellin** (see p103).

Four Days in and Around Milan

Day ❶

Arrive at **Santa Maria delle Grazie** (see p92) for an early reservation to see Leonardo's Last Supper (see pp12–13) then stroll to the basilica **Sant'Ambrogio** (see pp26–7) and the **Pinacoteca Ambrosiana** (see pp24–5). Following a quick lunch at **Princi** (see p88) head to Piazza Duomo to visit the stunning **Duomo** (see pp14–15) and wander among the pinnacles on

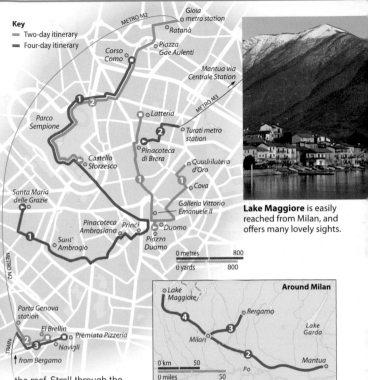

Key
— Two-day itinerary
— Four-day itinerary

Gioia metro station
Ratanà
Corso Como
Piazza Gae Aulenti
METRO M2
Mantua via Centrale Station
METRO M3
Parco Sempione
Latteria
Turati metro station
Castello Sforzesco
Pinacoteca di Brera
Quudrilutero d'Oro
Cova
Santa Maria delle Grazie
Galleria Vittorio Emanuele II
Pinacoteca Ambrosiana
Princi
Duomo
Sant' Ambrogio
Piazza Duomo
METRO M2

0 metres 800
0 yards 800

Lake Maggiore is easily reached from Milan, and offers many lovely sights.

Around Milan

Lake Maggiore
Bergamo
Lake Garda
Milan
Porta Genova station
El Brellin
Premiata Pizzeria
Navigli
TRAIN
↑ from Bergamo
Mantua
Po

0 km 50
0 miles 50

the roof. Stroll through the Brera to **Castello Sforzesco** *(see pp20–21)* and the adjacent **Parco Sempione** *(see p92)* and spend the evening among the exclusive bars and eateries of nearby Corso Como.

Day ❷
Make an early start at the **Pinacoteca di Brera** *(see pp16–19)* to enjoy more artistic marvels before leaving the city to spend the rest of the day in **Mantua** *(see pp34–5)*. Explore the churches and piazzas of the historic centre then hire a bicycle or join a boat tour to enjoy the city's lakes.

Day ❸
Today, head for **Bergamo** *(see pp32–3)*. Explore the sights of this lovely old town and take the funicular up to the ruined **Castello di San Vigilio** *(see p32)*. Get back to Milan for sunset over the **Navigli** canals *(see pp28–9)* and dinner at **Premiata Pizzeria** *(see p103)*.

Day ❹
Say goodbye to Milan and set off for **Lake Maggiore** *(see pp106–11)*, taking the ferry from **Stresa** *(see p109)* to the **Isole Borromee** *(see pp30–31)*. Stop first at Isola Bella for its extravagant gardens and the **Borromeo Palace** *(see p47)* then cross to Isola Madre for more exotic gardens and end up on pretty Isola dei Pescatori. Return to Stresa for dinner at **Osteria degli Amici** *(see p111)*.

Bergamo combines culture and charm.

Top 10 Milan and the Lakes Highlights

The city of Milan viewed from the roof of its magnificent Duomo

TOP 10 Milan and the Lakes Highlights

Milan is Italy's stylish economic powerhouse, backed up by an impressive cultural heritage of galleries, museums and ancient churches. Yet just a 40-minute train ride away lie azure lakes, lined with fishing villages, villas and laid-back resorts.

1 Leonardo's Last Supper

One of the most impressive works created by the ultimate Renaissance Man, it is sadly in an advanced state of deterioration now (see pp12–13).

2 Milan's Duomo

The world's largest Gothic cathedral took over 400 years to complete. It's a forest of pinnacles, flying buttresses and statues, with fantastic views from its roof (see pp14–15).

3 Pinacoteca di Brera

Northern Italy's greatest gallery displays masterpieces by Mantegna, Giovanni Bellini, Piero della Francesca, Raphael and Caravaggio (see pp16–19).

4 Castello Sforzesco

This sprawling 15th-century castle is now home to a wide range of collections, which include Michelangelo's final work, the Rondanini Pietà (see pp20–21).

5 Pinacoteca Ambrosiana
This cultural study centre, founded in the 17th century, contains works by Leonardo, Botticelli, Raphael and Caravaggio *(see pp24–5)*.

6 Sant'Ambrogio
This is one of the oldest churches in Milan, founded by the city's patron saint Ambrose in 379, with mosaics and carvings dating from the 4th century *(see pp26–7)*.

7 Navigli
Milan's picturesque canal district offers a vibrant evening scene. Boat trips and cycle paths offer an escape route from the busy city *(see pp28–9)*.

8 Isole Borromee, Lake Maggiore
Three verdant islands, one still a fishing village, the other two clad in the sumptuous villas and ornate gardens *(see pp30–31)*.

9 Bergamo
The perfect balance of small town charm and sophisticated culture, ancient streets and chic boutiques *(see pp32–3)*.

10 Mantua
Ringed on three sides by shallow lakes, the ancient seat of the Gonzaga dukes boasts Renaissance palaces by the likes of Mantegna and Romano *(see pp34–5)*.

TOP 10 ⭐ Leonardo's Last Supper

The Last Supper, Leonardo da Vinci's 1495–7 masterpiece, is a touchstone of Renaissance painting. Since the day it was finished, art students have journeyed to Milan to view the work, which takes up a refectory wall in a Dominican convent next to the church of Santa Maria delle Grazie. When writer Aldous Huxley called it "the saddest work of art in the world", he was referring not to the impact of the scene but to the fresco's fragile state of deterioration.

Leonardo da Vinci's remarkable depiction of the Last Supper

① Light
Note the brilliant effects of the interaction between the three sources of light – from the refectory itself, from windows painted in the background, and from the windows on the refectory's left wall.

② Coats of Arms Above Painting
The lunettes, above the fresco, were also painted by Leonardo. It seems he was as happy painting perfect leaves around the Sforza coats of arms as he was composing the vast scene below.

③ Example of Ageing
Montorfano's *Crucifixion* was painted in true *buon fresco*, but the now barely visible kneeling figures to the sides were added later on dry plaster – the same method Leonardo used.

NEED TO KNOW

MAP J3 ■ Tourist info: Piazza S Maria delle Grazie 2/Corso Magenta, Milan ■ 02-9280-0360 ■ www.vivaticket.it (tickets)

Open 8:15am–6:45pm Tue–Sun

Adm €10 plus €2 booking fee; free for EU citizens under 18, over 65 or disabled

■ Book well in advance, especially if visiting during the holidays.

■ Guided tours in English are at 9:30am and 3:30pm.

■ The informative audio guide will help explain why such a deteriorated fresco is so important.

■ On Via Magenta at via Carducci 13, Bar Magenta is a pleasing blend of Art Deco café and Guinness pub *(see p68)*.

5 Judas

Previously Judas was often painted across the table from everyone else. However, Leonardo's approach is more subtle, and instead he places the traitor right in the midst of the other disciples, snugly between Andrew and Peter **(left)**.

6 Groupings

Leonardo studied the effects of sound and physical waves. The groups of figures reflect the triangular Trinity concept (with Jesus at the centre) as well as the effect of a metaphysical shock wave, emanating out from Jesus and reflecting back from the walls as he reveals there is a traitor in their midst.

7 Reflections

The colours of the disciples' robes are reflected in the glasses and pewter plates on the table, heightening the illusion of reality.

A VANISHING FRESCO

Rather than paint in *buon fresco* (applying pigment to wet plaster so the colours bind with the base), Leonardo used oil paint on semi-dry plaster, causing it to deteriorate while still in progress. Napoleon's troops used the fresco for target practice, and World War II bombs blew off the roof. Restoration has removed centuries of over-painting and filled gaps with a pale wash.

4 Crucifixion on Opposite Wall

Most people spend so much time gazing at *The Last Supper* that they don't notice the 1495 fresco by Donato Montorfano on the opposite wall **(below)**, rich in colour and detail.

8 The Table

The table probably has the same sort of cloth and settings that the monks would have used, reinforcing the illusion that they were sharing their meals with Jesus and the Apostles.

9 "Halo" of Jesus

The medieval taste for halos is satisfied without sacrificing Renaissance realism: Christ is set in front of a window **(above)**, giving him the requisite nimbus without looking as if he's wearing a plate for a hat.

10 Perspective

The walls of the room in the painting appear to be continuations of the walls of the room you are in. The lines zoom in on Christ at the centre, which draws your eye towards his, helping to heighten the drama.

TOP 10 ⭐ Milan's Duomo

Milan's cathedral took almost 430 years to complete, from its 1386 inception to the finishing touches in 1813, and the builders stuck tenaciously to the Gothic style. It is the fifth-largest church in the world, with over 3,500 exterior statues, and is held up inside by 52 huge columns.

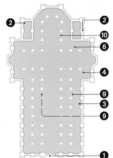

Façade ①
It wasn't until 1805–13 that the Neo-Gothic frontage, with its bronze doors and reliefs **(right)**, was finally built. The impressive central bronze door is by the Milanese sculptor Ludovico Pogliaghi.

③ Stained-Glass Windows
Dozens of stained-glass windows **(left)** create splashes of coloured light in the otherwise gloomy interior. The oldest, on the right aisle, date from 1470; the newest from 1988.

Milan's Duomo

② Ascent to Roof
Climb or take the lift to the roof to see the cathedral's remarkable Gothic crown of spires, gargoyles and statues – and for the views *(see p51)*.

NEED TO KNOW

MAP M4 ■ Piazza del Duomo, Milan ■ 02-7202-2656 ■ www.duomo milano.it

Cathedral: open 8am–7pm daily (last adm 6pm)

Roof: open 9am–7pm (to 10pm May–mid-Sep) daily (last adm one hour before), €13 by elevator, €9 by stairs (concs apply)

Museo del Duomo: open 10am–6pm Tue–Sun (last adm 5pm) €3 (concs apply)

■ You cannot enter if your shoulders are bare or your shorts or skirt rise above mid-thigh; bring a light shawl or two.

■ On clear days, the view from the roof stretches as far as the Alps.

■ You're spoilt for café choices, but nothing beats a Campari at the historic *Zucca (see pp68 and 88)*.

4 Funerary Monument to Gian Giacomo Medici

Leone Leoni created the 1560–63 tomb of a local mercenary general, including a life-sized bronze of him dressed in centurion armour.

8 Museo del Duomo

Here you'll find stained-glass windows and tapestries removed from the Duomo for safety; a masterpiece by Tintoretto, *The Infant Christ among the Doctors*; and wooden models of the Duomo.

10 Ambulatory and Crypt

The ambulatory is now open only to worshippers, but you can see a lovely example of a 14th-century Lombard sacristy door. Stairs nearby lead down into the crypt, where the body of St Charles Borromeo rests in a crystal coffin, and to the treasury, which is filled with elegant reliquaries and liturgical devices.

5 Battistero Paleocristiano

A stairway near the entrance leads down to excavations, which have uncovered traces of Roman baths dating from the 1st century BC, a baptistry from AD 287 and the remains of a 4th-century basilica.

9 Naves

The lofty interior (above) is a thicket of 52 pilasters ringed with statues of saints tucked into niches. The Gothic "tracery" on the vaulting of the four outer naves is actually ingenious *trompe l'oeil* paintings dating from the 16th century.

6 St Bartholomew Flayed

Marco d'Agrate's gruesome carving of 1562 shows the unfortunate saint with muscles and veins exposed and his flayed skin thrown jauntily over one shoulder.

7 La Madonnina

At the top of the Duomo's central spire, 108 m (354 ft) above ground level, the gilded copper "Little Madonna" has surveyed Milan's best panorama since 1774. Until 1995 she remained the highest point in the city.

LA FABBRICA DEL DUOMO

There is undoubtedly no better example of Milanese tenacity than the fact that their cathedral is a totally unspoilt example of the pure Gothic style, in spite of it taking a full 427 years to build. The generations of builders somehow ignored the siren calls of every new style that came along, from the Renaissance, then Baroque, to Neo-Classical. It is for this reason that the phrase *la fabbrica del Duomo*, "the building of the Duomo", in Milanese dialect – is still used to this day to refer to any job or enterprise that seems to take forever to complete.

TOP 10 ⭐ Pinacoteca di Brera

Milan's Brera is unique among Italy's major art galleries in that it isn't founded on the riches of the church or a noble family, but the policies of Napoleon, who suppressed churches across the region and took their treasures off to galleries and academies. Over the next two centuries, the collections grew to take in some of the best Renaissance-era painting from Northern Italy, representatives of the Venetian school and several giants of central Italy, including Raphael and Piero della Francesca.

1 Umberto Boccioni's Riot in the Galleria

In this painting of 1911 (**below**), the Milanese are depicted dashing for the doors of Zucca *(see p68)*. A companion work of 1910, *The City Rises*, is also here.

2 Tintoretto's Finding the Body of St Mark

Tintoretto uses his mastery of drama and light in this work of the 1560s to highlight the finding of the body of St Mark by Venetian merchants at the time of the Crusades.

3 Bellini's Virgin and Child

The Brera has two very different versions of Bellini's *Virgin and Child*. One is almost a Flemish-style portrait, painted when Bellini was 40. The other (**above**) is a luminous scene of colour and light, from 40 years later.

NEED TO KNOW

MAP M2 ■ Via Brera 28, Milan ■ 02-722-631; booking line 02-9280-0361 ■ www.pinacotecabrera.org

Open 8:30am–7:15pm Tue–Sun (last adm 6:30pm)

Adm; free for EU citizens under 18, over 65 or disabled

■ Make sense of the works on display with the excellent audio guides.

■ Cheap guided tours for any number of people are available on weekdays, but must be booked 2–3 days in advance.

■ Try the bars of the Brera district *(see p96)* for a post-gallery apéritif.

Pinacoteca di Brera

4 Gentile Fabriano's Valle Romita Polyptych

The Brera worked hard to reconstitute this altarpiece of 1410. The five main panels came with Napoleon; the other four were tracked down later.

8 Caravaggio's Supper at Emmaus

This 1605 work was Caravaggio's second painting of the Supper. The deep-black shadows and bright highlights create mood and tension.

9 Canaletto's Bacino di San Marco

The undisputed master of 18th-century Venetian cityscapes, Canaletto painted at least seven versions of this scene of St Mark's bell tower and the Doge's Palace.

10 Mantegna's Dead Christ

Mantegna was one of the Renaissance's greatest perspective virtuosos – this is his remarkable foreshortened masterpiece, which was painted in about 1500 **(below)**.

5 Piero della Francesca's Montefeltro Altarpiece

This 1472 scene **(above)** shows Piero's patron, the Duke of Montefeltro, kneeling in front of the Virgin and Child. Just a few months earlier, the duke's beloved wife had given birth to a male heir, but the child had tragically died within weeks.

6 Raphael's Marriage of the Virgin

In this early (1504) painting depicting the Virgin Mary's terrestrial marriage to Joseph, Raphael took the idea and basic layout from his Umbrian master Perugino, tweaking it with a perfected single-point perspective based on mathematical rules.

7 Francesco Hayez's The Kiss

This much-loved 1859 scene **(left)** – painted when Hayez was 68 – was intended by the artists as an allegory of the passionate struggle for independence at the time of the Risorgimento.

THE PALACE OF BRERA

Built from 1591 to 1658 as a Jesuit college, the late-Baroque Palazzo di Brera was not finished until 1774. The palace's vast courtyard centres around a bronze statue of Napoleon presented in the guise of Mars. The statue, commissioned in 1807, was installed 52 years later in 1859.

⭐10 The Brera Collections

Coronation of the Virgin Polyptych by
Andrea di Bartolo e Giorgio di Andrea

1 13th-Century Paintings (Rooms II–IV)

Italian art simply wouldn't be the same without the naturalism, bright colours and emotive qualities that Giotto brought to the world of painting, and his influence is clear in works such as *Three Scenes from the Life of St Columba* by Giovanni Baronzio of Rimini. Other works here trace the Gothic style from Central Italy (Ambrogio Lorenzetti and Andrea di Bartolo) to Venice (Lorenzo Veneziano and Jacopo Bellini). The best works are Ambrogio Lorenzetti's *Virgin and Child* and Gentile da Fabriano's *Crucifixion*.

The Brera Collections

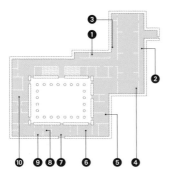

2 Jesi Collection of 20th Century Art (Room X)

When Maria Jesi donated her impressive art hoard in 1976, the Brera became the first major museum in Italy to acquire a significant 20th-century collection. Boccioni's *Riot in the Galleria* is highlighted on p16; other master-works are by Morandi, Severini, Modigliani, Picasso and Braque.

Modigliani's *Portrait of Moisè Kisling*

3 Venetian Renaissance (Rooms VI; IX; XIV; XIX)

It is the art of Venice that steals the show at the Brera, and the bulk of the museum's important works fill these ten rooms: Mantegna's *Dead Christ* (see p17) and numerous superlative works by his brother-in-law Giovanni Bellini. It all culminates in the brushy, stormy, wondrously lit and intriguingly coloured scenes of Venice's High Renaissance trio: Tintoretto, Titian and Paolo Veronese.

4 Lombard Renaissance (Rooms XII; XV)

The stars of the Lombard section are the 16th-century Campi clan from Cremona, painters inspired by Raphael and, above all Leonardo da Vinci. Tiny Room XIX is devoted to

Madonna della Candeletta by
Carlo Crivelli

the heirs of the Leonardo revolution:
Il Bergognone and Bernardino Luini.

⑤ Marchese Renaissance (Rooms XXI–XIII; XXII)

These rooms feature Flemish-inspired artists and 15th-century painters from the central Marches province. The latter took local art from the post-Giotto Gothicism into a courtly Early Renaissance style, exemplified by Carlo Crivelli.

⑥ Tuscan Renaissance (Rooms XXIV–XXVII)

The few paintings here are stunners: Piero's *Montefeltro Altarpiece* and Raphael's *Marriage of the Virgin (see p17)*, alongside works by Bramante, Signorelli and Bronzino.

The Chanter by Bramante

⑦ 17th-Century Bolognese Renaissance (Room XXVIII)

As Florence and Rome got swept away with Mannerist fantasies and experiments, Bolognese artists held the line on Classical Renaissance ideals. In this room we see Ludovico Caracci, Il Guercino and Guido Reni engaged in an ever more crystalline and reductive naturalistic style.

Abraham casting out Hagar and Ishmael by Guercino

⑧ Caravaggio and his Followers (Room XXIX)

Caravaggio's use of harsh contrast in paintings such as the *Supper at Emmaus (see p17)* influenced a generation of painters. The works of some of the best of them – Mattia Preti, Jusepe de Ribera and Orazio Gentileschi – are on display here too.

⑨ Baroque and Rococo (Rooms XXX–XXXVI)

In the late 16th century, Italy moved from Renaissance naturalism to the more ornate style of the Baroque, with Daniele Crespi and Pietro da Cortona to the fore. The Baroque fed off its own overblown conventions until it became Rococo, a lavish style that was heralded by Tiepolo and Giuseppe Maria Crespi.

⑩ 19th-Century Painting (Rooms XXXVII; XXXVIII)

There's not so much of interest in these final rooms, save Francesco Hayez's monumental scenes and the pseudo-Impressionist Macchiaioli school (Fattori, Segantini and Lega).

TOP 10 ★ Castello Sforzesco

This massive, rectangular bastion in Milan is actually a complex of fortresses, castles and towers begun in 1451 for Francesco Sforza, largely restored in 1893–1904, and again after massive World War II damage. Its many collections include art and sculpture from the early Middle Ages to the 18th century, decorative arts, musical instruments, Oriental art and archaeology.

3 Bellini's Madonna and Child

This is an early Bellini **(left)**, painted in 1468–70, with touching detail. Mary wears a pearl-trimmed pink shawl, and Jesus gazes at a lemon.

4 Bellini's Poet Laureate

The attribution of this portrait, painted in 1475, has wavered between Bellini and Antonella da Messina.

1 Michelangelo's Rondanini Pietà

Michelangelo started his career with a *Pietà* carved at the age of 25 (now in St Peter's, Rome). He was famous for not finishing his statues, but in this case it was not his fault. At the age of 89 he had a stroke while working on this piece.

5 Mantegna's Madonna in Glory

Bellini's brother-in-law painted this magnificent altarpiece for a Verona church in 1497, making it one of his final works. Age and experience combine to yield a solid, naturalistic approach.

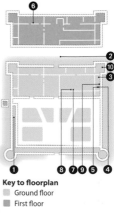

2 Parco Sempione

This 1893 public park **(below)** northwest of the castle is central Milan's largest green space. Many of its structures are fine early Art Nouveau *(see p92)*.

Castello Sforzesco

Key to floorplan
Ground floor
First floor

⑧ Cappella Ducale

The Ducal Chapel has frescoes **(left)** painted in 1472 by Stefano de Fedeli and Bonifacio Bembo for Galeazzo Maria Sforza, including a *Resurrection* and an *Annunciation*.

TOMB OF GASTON DE FOIX

In 1510, King Francis I ordered a tomb for the hero. Bambaia sculpted an effigy of the warrior, lying in state. When the French pulled out of Milanese affairs in 1522, work on it stopped and pieces were sold off, winding up here, in the Ambrosiana *(see p24)*, in Turin and in London.

⑩ Sala delle Asse

The "Plank Hall" was decorated in 1498 by Leonardo da Vinci with a trompe l'oeil of intricate vines on the vaulted ceiling. The only bit we can be sure is original is a monochrome sketch of a twisting root, on the wall between two windows.

NEED TO KNOW

MAP K2

Castello Sforzesco: Piazza Castello, Milan; 02-8846-3700; open 7am–7:30pm daily (to 6pm in winter); www.milanocastello.it

Musei Civici: 02-8846-3703; open 9am–5:30pm Tue–Sun; adm €5 (free from 2pm Tue, from 4:30pm Wed–Sun and for under-18s)

- Ask about special tours that explore many non-museum sections of the castle and are usually closed to the public.

- Snack vans on-site are overpriced, and the nearest bars are best avoided. Head down Via Dante to the café at No. 15, where you can enjoy panini and gelato.

⑥ Trivulzio Tapestries

The *Tapestries of the Twelve Months* **(above)** were designed by Bramantino in 1503 and named for the man who commissioned them, Gian Giacomo Trivulzio.

⑨ Bronzino's Lorenzo Lenzi

A Mannerist painter at the Medici court in Florence, Bronzino's delicate portrait shows a sensitivity to his subject's youthful restlessness.

⑦ Funerary Monument for Gaston de Foix

Gaston de Foix was ruler of the French Milan Duchy and posthumous hero of the 1512 Battle of Ravenna. His tomb **(above)** was broken up and sold *(see box)*.

⭐ Pinacoteca Ambrosiana

Local Cardinal Federico Borromeo founded this library (of some 36,000 manuscripts and over 750,000 prints) and painting gallery in Milan in 1603 after a formative time spent in Rome's artistic circles. It was (and is) a place in which to study theological issues via academic tomes and works of art, a truly Renaissance mix of religion, intellectualism and aesthetics. There are paintings by such greats as Tiepolo, Francesco Hayez and Jan Brueghel.

4 Bassano's Rest on the Flight into Egypt

The Venetian master Jacopo Bassano was turning to a densely coloured palette, rich in contrasting tones, when he produced this work **(left)** in 1547.

5 Bambaia's Detail from the Tomb of Gaston de Foix

The Milanese sculptor carved this series of small marble panels **(below)** with figures surrounded by military accoutrements and mythological creatures, all in extraordinary high relief. Most of the monument is in the Castello Sforzesco *(see pp20–21)*.

1 Titian's Adoration of the Magi

This courtly tumble of the three kings kissing the toes of baby Jesus in his manger was part of Federico Borromeo's original collection, a complex work from 1560 that the cardinal described as "a school for painters".

2 Leonardo's Portrait of a Musician

This portrait, quasi-Flemish in pose and detail, yet glowing with a sense of human psychology typical of Leonardo, has been said to depict various individuals, but it most likely represents a musician of the Sforza court. It is almost certainly by Leonardo, but has probably been retouched over the years.

NEED TO KNOW

MAP L4 ▪ Piazza Pio XI 2, Milan ▪ 02-806-921 ▪ www.ambrosiana.it

Open 10am–6pm Tue–Sun (last adm 5:30pm)

Adm €15, concs €10

▪ Just round the corner, on Via Spadari, you will find Gastronomia Peck *(see p87)*, one of Italy's best food emporia and oversized *tavole calde* (snack bars/cafés).

3 Botticelli's Madonna del Padiglione

Angels pull back a rich canopy to reveal a scene of Mary and Jesus in a pastoral setting. This work dates from the 1490s, after Botticelli's religious crisis turned him from the mythological scenes of his youth.

6 Raphael's Cartoon for School of Athens

This is the preparatory drawing for Raphael's famous fresco of Greek philosophers, which features the faces of Renaissance artists.

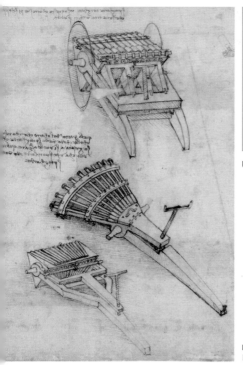

Pinacoteca Ambrosiana

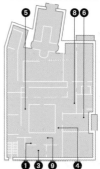

Key to floorplan
Ground floor

⑦ Leonardo's Codex Atlantico

Reproductions of pages from these oversized tomes **(above)** are on display inside glass-topped tables. They are filled with Leonardo da Vinci's sketches.

⑧ Bril's Landscape with St Paul

This is quite the most dramatic of the over half-dozen Bril works on display, showcasing how Bril managed to work with the early 17th-century's most popular sacred scenes but set them in his beloved, intricately executed landscape form.

⑨ Luini's Holy Family

If this looks familiar, it is because, especially early on, Luini was almost slavishly devoted to the manner of his master Leonardo da Vinci, and this painting is based on a famous drawing by him.

⑩ Caravaggio's Basket of Fruit

This still life **(below)** shows how Caravaggio was, even at the age of 25, perfecting the hyperrealism he would soon apply to large canvases and more complex scenes.

TOP 10 ⭐ Sant'Ambrogio

One of Milan's oldest basilicas (founded by St Ambrose in 379) served as a model for most of the city's early medieval churches. It was enlarged in the 9th century, and what we see today dates largely from 1080 (albeit with later reconstructions). It instantly became Milan's most beloved house of worship when the wildly popular (and future patron saint) Ambrose was buried here in 397. Everything is signposted in Italian and English.

1 Golden Altar
The master goldsmith Volvinio crafted the magnificent "golden altar" in 835 **(left)**. The Life of Christ is in gold leaf on the front, and the Life of St Ambrose in gilded silver on the back.

2 Façade
The austere but balanced façade **(right)** consists of five arches fitted under the peaked roofline. It is flanked by two mismatched towers: the Monks' Tower on the right, dating from the 9th century, and the Canons' Tower on the left from 1144.

3 Sarcophagus of Stilicho
This late Roman-era sarcophagus preceded the pulpit, which was built around it. The tomb is aligned with the original walls, while the pulpit aligns itself with the nave.

4 Bergognone's Redeemer
This limpid, late 15th-century Renaissance scene of the Risen Christ **(right)** was originally positioned on the wall to the right of the altar (where its painted trompe l'oeil architecture was far more suited). It was later moved to the first chapel on the left.

NEED TO KNOW

MAP K4

Sant'Ambrogio: Piazza Sant'Ambrogio 15; 02-8645-0895; open 7:30am–12:30pm & 2:30–7pm Mon–Sat, 7:30am–1pm & 3–8pm Sun

Sacello di San Vittore, Ciel d'Oro: open 9:30–11:45am & 2:30–6pm daily; adm €2

Museo della Basilica: open 10am–noon, 2:30–5:30pm daily, (no access during Mass); adm €2

■ The best of the more portable objects from the church treasury and small museum are now displayed in the Museo Diocesano *(see p100).*

■ Walk northwest to visit the Art Nouveau café-pub Bar Magenta *(see p68).*

Sant'Ambrogio

5 Atrium

The elongated atrium **(below)** between the entrance and the church, was built from 1088 to 1099 using columns with 6th-century capitals of fantastical scenes.

8 Sacello di San Vittore in Ciel d'Oro

Sant'Ambrogio was built next to a Paleochristian cemetery and a chapel decorated in the 5th century with a dome of gold mosaics. The basilica eventually grew to include the chapel.

9 Pulpit

This composite of 11th- and early 12th-century Romanesque relief panels was saved after the church ceiling collapsed in 1196 and reconstructed into this magnificent pulpit.

6 Ciborium

This altar canopy sits at the centre of the presbytery. Its four ancient Roman columns support a canopy of four 10th-century Lombard stucco reliefs.

7 Serpent Column

Just on the inside of the third pier on the left stands a short column topped by a curlicue of a bronze serpent, a 10th-century Byzantine work (although local legend says it's the serpent cast by Moses).

10 Apse Mosaics

The vast, colourful mosaic depicting Christ Pantocrater **(above)** was pieced together between the 4th and 8th centuries, though bits were touched up or redone between the 17th and 20th centuries.

TOP 10 ⭐ Navigli

Colourful bars and restaurants make Milan's Navigli canal district one of the city's favourites for an evening out. In the past, however, the area was a bustling transport hub with links to lakes Maggiore and Como. Dating from the 12th century, Milan's system of canals is Europe's most ancient – even Leonardo da Vinci contributed, coming up with an ingenious system of locks to solve the problem of water-level changes. Today, tranquil canalside paths lead from Navigli out of town through the countryside and to nearby villages.

1 Cycle Paths
Canalside paths (below) are perfect for a relaxed cycle ride. Hire a bike and explore the Navigli district or keep going along the canal to leave the city behind and discover nearby villages such as pretty Gaggiano.

3 Boat Trips
A 55-minute trip takes in most of the main sights of the Naviglio Grande and the docks. Other itineraries include NavigarMangiando, which includes dinner at an out-of-town canalside trattoria.

4 Vicolo dei Lavandai
Canal water fills the picturesque roofed washerwomen's area, still fitted with stone washboards, at this charming corner of Naviglio Grande. The adjacent building, now the El Brellin restaurant (see p103), once sold brushes and soap.

Canalside scene in the lovely Navigli district

2 Santa Maria delle Grazie al Naviglio
This imposing Neo-Gothic church (below) offers an oasis of peace at the heart of the lively bars and restaurants of the Naviglio Grande. It was built at the start of the 20th century over a previous one.

5 Arts and Crafts
As you walk along the canals you'll come across a stimulating selection of Bohemian-chic boutiques, design studios and arts and crafts workshops, many based in picturesque interior courtyards.

6 Naviglio Martesana
Only two of Milan's canals (Naviglio Grande and Pavese) meet here. Naviglio Martesana, with a lovely canalside path, starts just northeast of the centre, ending at Trezzo sull'Adda (see p58).

8 San Cristoforo sul Naviglio

Two churches, built side-by-side and dating from the 12th and 15th centuries, have been annexed to make up this attractive complex situated by the bridge of the same name. The walls feature several frescoes **(left)**, both internally and externally.

NAVIGLIO GRANDE

Naviglio Grande is the oldest of Milan's canals. Work began in 1177 and was completed 100 years later. It links the historic centre to the Ticino River and on to Lake Maggiore and Switzerland. The curious iron footbridge between Via Casale and Paoli dates from 1905.

7 Aperitivo Time

Each of the many bars of Navigli has its own character but they all lay out an elaborate feast of bar snacks every evening at *aperitivo* time. Buy a drink and help yourself from the buffet.

9 Darsena

Restoration work at Milan's former docks has uncovered previously hidden canals. There are street food stalls in summer and a colourful Christmas market in winter.

NEED TO KNOW

MAP J6–K6

Santa Maria delle Grazie al Naviglio: Alzaia Naviglio Grande 34

Boat Trips: www. naviglilombardi.it

San Cristoforo sul Naviglio: Via San Cristoforo 3

Antiques Market: www. navigliogrande.mi.it

■ The El Brellin restaurant *(see p103)* also has a bar; its aperitivo time (see above) starts at 6pm each evening and there's often live jazz in summer.

■ Happy hour in Milan does not mean you'll get discounted drinks – on the contrary, prices are often higher than usual, but the buffet of bar snacks is included.

10 Antiques Market

A treasure trove of items from yesteryear fills the multitude of stalls which set up along the Naviglio Grande canal on the last Sunday of each month **(above)**. Other regular open-air events include a canalside art show that takes place in mid-May.

TOP 10 ⭐ Isole Borromee, Lake Maggiore

This cluster of islands near Stresa has been shaped by the Borromeo family. In the 16th and 17th centuries they turned Bella and Madre into vast garden-and-palace complexes; Isola Bella is the most striking, while Isola Madre, the largest, has landscaped botanical gardens that are a joy to explore. The third island, Isola dei Pescatori, is an authentic fishing village, while the tiny Scoglio della Malghera has little more than a beach.

1 Tapestries in the Palace, Isola Bella

This detail-rich series of 16th-century Flemish works **(above)** is based on that popular theme for medieval tapestries: the unicorn (which is also a Borromeo heraldic totem).

2 Borromeo Tombs, Isola Bella

The "Private Chapel" was built in 1842–4 as a mausoleum for a pair of late Gothic/early Renaissance family tombs as well as the 1522 Monument to the Birago Brothers, carved by Renaissance master Bambaia.

3 Borromeo Palace, Isola Bella

The vast palace and its grounds **(below)** dominate the island. Largely 17th century, it wasn't finished until 1959. The sumptuous rooms have stucco ceilings and are filled with Murano chandeliers and fine art.

4 Kashmir Cypress, Isola Madre

Europe's largest cypress spreads its 200-year-old, weeping Oriental strands of needles over a Villa Borromeo courtyard.

5 Grottoes, Isola Bella

Artificial caves were all the rage in the 18th century **(below)**. They were decorated with intricate pebble-work in black-and-white patterns.

6 Sala di Musica in the Palace, Isola Bella

In April 1935, Mussolini met in this room with Laval of France and Ramsay MacDonald of Britain in an attempt to stave off World War II.

7 Isola dei Pescatori

The Borromei largely left this island alone when they were converting its neighbours, leaving a working fishing village. Wander the cobbled lanes, visit the 11th-century church and stop at one of the many cateries.

8 Gardens, Isola Bella

This pyramid of terraces **(above)** is topped by a unicorn, the edges lined by ornate, statue-laden balustrades. White peacocks strut over the clipped lawns.

9 Botanical Gardens, Isola Madre

The lush and extensive gardens around the Villa Borromeo are filled with exotic flora. Since the 19th century they have been famed for the flowering of many azaleas, rhododendrons and camellias.

THE BORROMEO FAMILY

The Borromeo clan fled political intrigue in Tuscany for Milan in 1395, where they funded the rise of the Visconti. They weathered the era's turbulent political storms, married wisely, and associated with the Sforza while slowly acquiring control of Lake Maggiore. The Borromeo family still owns these islands.

10 Villa Borromeo, Isola Madre

This summer villa was built largely between 1518 and 1585. Today it is a museum with manne-quins in Borromeo livery and paraphernalia from puppet theatres.

NEED TO KNOW

MAP A2 ■ Access is from the ferry docks at Stresa *(see p109)* ■ www.isoleborromee.it

Isola Bella: 0323-30-556; open late Mar–Oct: 9am–5:30pm daily; adm €16, under-16s €8.50

Isola Madre: 0323-31-261; open late Mar–Oct: 9am–5:30pm daily; adm €13, under-16s €6.50 Exact dates vary annually; check website

■ Buy discounted island admission tickets along with your ferry ticket at the Stresa docks.

■ Isola Bella's gardens remain open all day and access is via the palazzo.

■ There are many cafés on Isola Bella's quay. Café Lago serves good panini, snacks, coffee, beer and wine.

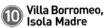

2 km (1.2 miles)

Isola dei Pescatori

Scoglio della Malghera

Isole Borromee, Lake Maggiore

Isola Bella

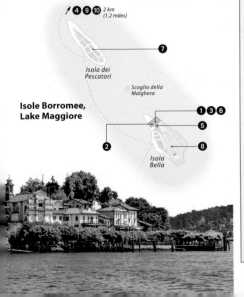

TOP 10 ⭐ Bergamo

One of Northern Italy's surprising gems, Bergamo mixes medieval charm with cultural sophistication. Bergamo has been a split-level town since Roman times, when a *civitas* (today's medieval Upper Town) perched on top of the hill and a *suburbia* (the now modernized Lower Town) spread into the plain.

1 Galleria dell' Accademia Carrara

This gallery **(above)**, housed in a Neo-Classical building, has over 1,800 works of art including Mantegna's *Madonna and Child* and Raphael's *Saint Sebastian*.

3 Piazza Vecchia

In the Upper Town (Città Alta), one of Northern Italy's most theatrical squares **(right)** is surrounded by retro-medieval stone buildings, Renaissance palaces, a 12th-century tower and several historic cafés.

2 Castello di San Vigilio

Constructed by the town's Venetian lords in the 16th and 17th centuries, the castle in the hamlet of San Vigilio has been reduced to romantic ruins. The garden boasts fine views.

4 Galleria d'Arte Moderna e Contemporanea

Bergamo's modern art gallery features changing exhibitions alongside a permanent collection which includes works by some of Italy's key 20th-century painters.

5 Via Colleoni

The main drag of Bergamo's Upper Town is lined with shops and bars, modest medieval palaces and churches, tiny squares and half-timbered houses. It's closed to most traffic, and busy every evening.

NEED TO KNOW

MAP D3

Tourist Information: IAT Lower Town, Piazzale Papa Giovanni XXIII, 57, 035-210-204; IAT Upper Town, Viale Gombito 13, 035-242-226; www.visitbergamo.net

Galleria dell'Accademia Carrara: open 9:30am–5:30pm Wed–Mon; adm €10

Castello di San Vigilio: open 10am–6pm (Nov–Feb: to 4pm) daily

Galleria d'Arte Moderna e Contemporanea: open 10am–7pm Wed–Sun (to 10pm Thu); adm €6

Museo del 500 Veneto: open 9:30am–1pm, 2:30–6pm Tue–Sun (Jun–Sep: all day Sat, Sun & hols); adm €5

Basilica di Santa Maria Maggiore: open 9am–12:30pm (to 1pm Sun & hols) & 2:30–5pm Mon–Sat, 3–6pm Sun & hols

Museo Donizettiano: open 9:30am–1pm, 2:30–6pm Tue–Sun (Oct–May: closed weekday pm); adm €3

■ A funicular connects the upper and lower towns.

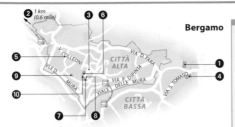

Bergamo

⑨ Museo Donizettiano

The museum's collection contains the original sheet music, piano **(below)** and memorabilia of Bergamo's famous composer Gaetano Donizetti (1797–1848). He died of syphilis in the very bed that's on display here.

⑥ Museo del 500 Veneto

This museum in the Palazzo Podesta explores life in the 16th century, taking the visitor on a virtual journey from Venice to Bergamo.

⑦ Basilica di Santa Maria Maggiore

Inside the basilica **(left)**, every inch of ceiling is covered with frescoes. The gorgeous, early 16th-century, inlaid wood panels fronting the choir are by Lorenzo Lotto.

⑧ Piazza del Duomo

This square is dominated by elaborate Bergamasco architecture: Santa Maria Maggiore, the Capella Colleoni and a fanciful 1340 baptistry.

⑩ Cappella Colleoni

The anchor of the twinned Piazza Vecchia and Piazza del Duomo is this magnificent Renaissance chapel devoted to Bergamo's warrior-lord Bartolomeo Colleoni. In pink-and-white patterned marble, it is covered with reliefs and Rococo frescoes.

TOP 10 ⭐ Mantua

This town is known for its fine palaces, masterpieces by Mantegna and Giulio Romano and its position surrounded on three sides by wide, shallow, swamp-edged lakes. These man-made lakes make the area humid in summer and rather damp and chilly in winter, creating a slight air of melancholy. The city makes up for this, however, with its cobbled lanes, attractive squares and cultural history: it was the birthplace of the poet Virgil and the setting of Verdi's opera *Rigoletto*.

1 Duomo

The cathedral has an 18th-century façade **(below)**, and its interior, reconstructed from the Gothic original by Giulio Romano, is an imitation of Paleochristian basilicas.

3 Palazzo Ducale

Delights in the Gonzagas' rambling fortress-palace include tapestries by Raphael and Mantegna's *Camera degli Sposi* frescoes (1465–74).

Mantua

2 Casa del Mantegna

Mantua's most famous artist, Andrea Mantegna (1431–1506), custom-built this house and studio in 1465–74. It includes a circular courtyard and a portrait of himself by his fellow-artist and friend, Titian.

4 Piazza Broletto

Just north of the arcaded Piazza delle Erbe is this tiny square, hemmed in by medieval buildings including the 1227 *broletto* (town hall).

5 Basilica di Sant'Andrea

Lord Lodovico Gonzaga commissioned this basilica in 1470 from Leon Battista Alberti, its façade is a highly original take on Classicism. The tomb of Mantegna is in the first chapel on the left.

6 Teatro Scientifico Bibiena

This jewel-box of a late Baroque theatre **(above)** is named after the architect who designed it, and was inaugurated in 1770 with a concert by Mozart, then a 13-year-old prodigy.

7 Piazza delle Erbe

Piazza delle Erbe **(below)** is a lively urban space, lined by arcades, filled with a food market each morning, and ringed by fascinating ancient buildings.

9 Palazzo d'Arco

This Renaissance *palazzo*, later remodelled in Neo-Classical style, includes the exquisite 1520 Sala dello Zodiaco, frescoed with astrological signs, in an original 15th-century wing.

10 Palazzo Te

Giulio Romano's Mannerist masterpiece is an ingenious interplay of spacious open courts, sweeping wings and discreet gardens. Built in 1525, it was frescoed largely by Romano.

8 Rotonda di San Lorenzo

This rotund church is a relic from an earlier age, built in 1082 and retaining scraps of medieval fresco in its otherwise pleasantly bare brick interior.

Mantua, viewed from across a lake

BOAT TOURS

The Gonzagas widened the Mincio River, setting their city within three defensive lakes. Now the protected homes of waterfowl and of Italy's highest concentration of fish, they're at their best in May and June. Boat tours are available.

NEED TO KNOW
MAP H6

Tourist Information: Piazza Mantegna 6; www.turismo.mantova.it

Duomo: open 7am–noon & 3–7pm daily

Casa del Mantegna: open 10am–12:30pm, 3–6pm Wed–Sun

Palazzo Ducale: open 8:15am–7:15pm Tue–Sun; adm €12 (free first Sun of the month)

Basilica di Sant'Andrea: open 8am–noon & 3–7pm Mon–Fri, 10:30am–noon & 3–6pm Sat, 11:45am–12:15pm & 3–6pm Sun

Teatro Scientifico Bibiena: open 10am–1pm & 3–6pm Tue–Fri, 10am–6pm Sat, Sun & hols; adm €2

Rotonda di San Lorenzo: open 10am–1pm & 3–6pm Mon–Fri, 10am–7pm Sat & Sun; donation

Palazzo d'Arco: open 9:30am–1pm & 2:30–6pm Tue–Sun; adm €7

Palazzo Te: open 9am–6:30pm Tue–Sun, 1–6pm Mon; adm €12

Boat Tours: Motonavi Andes Negrini, 0376-322-875; Navi Andes, 0376-324-506

The Top 10 of Everything

Opulent interior of the historic La Scala opera house in Milan

Moments in History

① 298–283 BC: Third Samnite War

The Po Valley and land to the north, once called Cisalpine Gaul, was a Celtic province that often found itself up against Rome. Its alliance with the Samnites failed, and Rome then pushed its boundary north of the Po.

② AD 313: Edict of Milan

During Rome's decline Milan became the capital of the Western Roman Empire. Constantine, holding court here in 313, made Christianity the official religion, setting a new course for European history.

③ 572: Fall of Pavia to Lombards

In the 5th century barbarian tribes overran the disintegrating Roman Empire. The Germanic Lombards took Pavia in 572 and settled in the Po Valley, expanding across the north. The Byzantines and Charlemagne eventually trounced them, and the region dissolved into a network of city-states that lasted throughout the Middle Ages.

④ 1176: Lombard League Defeats Barbarossa

When Swabian Emperor Frederick I (Barbarossa) levelled Milan and set up his own puppet mayors, the area's city-states banded together as the Lombard League and, with papal support, forced Barbarossa to reinstate their autonomy.

Fresco showing the Battle of Desio

⑤ 1277: Ottone Visconti Defeats the Torriani

Archbishop Visconti overthrew the leading Torriani family at the Battle of Desio in 1277. Under 160 years of Visconti rule, Milan extended its hegemony over much of the north.

⑥ 1450: Francesco Sforza Comes to Power

The last Visconti died in 1447. His illegitimate daughter couldn't inherit the title but was married to Francesco Sforza. Milan hired Sforza to defend it from Venetian power-grabbers, but he cut a deal with Venice, split up the territory and made himself duke.

Lombard League battles Barbarossa

7 1499: The Sforza Cede Milan to France

Francesco's son Galeazzo Maria was murdered in 1476, and power passed to Galeazzo's brother Lodovico. He ushered the Renaissance into Milan, inviting the likes of Leonardo da Vinci to his court, but in 1499 ceded control to Louis XII. Milan continued to change hands until Austria took over in 1706.

8 1848: Cinque Giornate Revolt

The 19th-century Risorgimento (unification movement) inspired the Milanese to rise up, on 18 March, for five days, with their victory triggering the demise of Austrian rule. By 1859 King Vittorio Emanuele II controlled Lombardy: he sent General Garibaldi off to conquer the rest of the peninsula, forming a new kingdom – Italy.

Cinque Giornate riots in Milan

9 1945: Mussolini Executed

Mussolini's Fascist regime ended after his alliance with Hitler put Italy on the losing side of World War II. As the Allies drew closer, Mussolini fled with his mistress. They were caught by partisans and their bodies were strung up on Milan's Piazzale Loreto.

10 1990: Lombard League Wins Local Elections

Northern resentment of sharing wealth with the poorer south led to the Lombard League, which came to prominence in 1990. Re-dubbed the Northern League, in 2001 it gained power as part of the Forza Italia coalition (now known as Popolo della Libertà) led by Silvio Berlusconi.

TOP 10 HISTORICAL FIGURES

Coronation of Gian Galeazzo Visconti

1 St Ambrose (334–97)
Milan's bishop and patron saint put down the Arian heresy and helped establish Church autonomy.

2 St Augustine (354–430)
St Ambrose's star pupil, Augustine of Hippo was an African-born philosopher.

3 Theodolinda (500s)
Lombard queen who converted her populace to orthodox Christianity.

4 Gian Galeazzo Visconti (1378–1402)
This conqueror of vast territories was the first Milan ruler to be honoured with the title of Duke of the city.

5 Lodovico "Il Moro" Sforza (1452–1508)
"The Moor" ruled Milan's Renaissance court but ceded to France, later siding against the French and being exiled.

6 St Charles Borromeo (1538–84)
The crusading anti-heretic archbishop carried out often brutal Counter-Reformation ideals in the north.

7 Antonio Stradivari (1644–1737)
The greatest luthier (violin maker) who ever lived learned his craft in his birthplace city of Cremona.

8 Alessandro Volta (1745–1827)
This Como physicist invented the battery in 1800 and gave his name to the electrical unit.

9 Benito Mussolini (1883–1945)
Known as "Il Duce" (the Leader), Mussolini founded the Fascist Party in Milan in 1919, and ruled Italy from 1922 until 1943.

10 Giò Ponti (1891–1979)
Ponti was an important architect (Pirelli Tower, Torre Branca), industrial designer and furniture designer.

🔟 Churches

Santa Maria delle Grazie's lofty nave

1 Santa Maria delle Grazie, Milan

Each year, hundreds of thousands of people visit Leonardo da Vinci's *Last Supper* fresco in the adjacent refectory *(see pp12–13)*, but only a few bother with the lovely church itself. Make the effort, though, if you can: its architecture shows the stylistic changeover, from austere Gothic to Classical Renaissance, that marked the end of the 15th century. The art here is among Milan's best, including the rare *sgraffito* (etched designs) restored in the tribune *(see p92)*.

2 Basilica di Sant'Andrea, Mantua

Built to house a vial of Christ's blood, this basilica was created by some of Italy's finest architectural talents. Leon Battista Alberti, the great Renaissance theorist, designed it in 1470; Giulio Romano, a founder of Mannerism, enlarged it in 1530; and Baroque master Filippo Juvarra added the magnificent dome in 1732. Lovely frescoes cover the barrel-vaulted interior *(see pp34–5)*.

3 San Lorenzo Maggiore, Milan

Dating from the 4th century, this church is still pretty much Roman in its rotund design, although it was rebuilt several times in the Middle Ages. Roman columns line the front, and within are some of the oldest and best-preserved examples of post-Roman art in Northern Italy: 1,600-year-old Paleochristian mosaics *(see p99)*.

4 Sant'Ambrogio, Milan

St Ambrose himself, Milan's 4th-century bishop, inaugurated this church, which was overhauled in the 11th and 12th centuries. Highlights include a quiet entry atrium, Dark Age mosaics glittering in the apse, and medieval features *(see pp26–7)*.

5 Duomo, Milan

Milan's most famous landmark is the fifth-largest church in the world and a testament to Milanese persistence. The cathedral's most startling feature is its extraordinary roof, which boasts 135 spires, innumerable statues and gargoyles, and from which there are views of the Alps on a clear day *(see pp14–15)*.

Milan's Duomo

6 Sant'Eustorgio, Milan

Ignore the insipid 19th-century façade – the church behind was founded in the 4th century. Behind the altar is the Cappella Portinari. It was designed locally, but so superbly did it embody early Renaissance Florentine ideals that it was for a long time attributed to Brunelleschi or Michelozzo. The chapel's masterpieces are the 1486 frescoes by Vicenzo Foppa (see p100).

7 Certosa di Pavia

MAP C5 ■ **Via del Monumento 4, Pavia** ■ **0382-925-613** ■ **Open Apr: 9–11:30am, 2:30–5:30pm Tue–Sun (May–Sep: to 6pm); Oct–Mar: 9–11:30am, 2:30–6pm Tue–Sat (to 5pm Sun)**

Gian Galeazzo Visconti had this vast, gorgeous Charterhouse built in 1396 as a lavishly decorated home for a group of Carthusian monks, but more importantly to ensure his ruling clan would have a family burial chapel of grand proportions and extravagant artistic merit.

8 Cappella Colleoni, Bergamo

Condottiere Bartolomeo Colleoni was a redoubtable mercenary general who, as a reward for his services, received Bergamo as his own fiefdom. Colleoni demolished a church sacristy to make his own tomb, hiring the sculptor Giovanni Antonio Amadeo to decorate it with a complex allegory of biblical and Classical reliefs plus a horse-mounted effigy of himself for the sepulchre inside (see p32).

9 Santa Maria presso San Satiro, Milan

Though the main entrance is on Via Torino, walk up Via Speronari to see an 11th-century bell tower and the exterior of a tiny Renaissance chapel. Turn right on Via Falcone for the Renaissance-meets-Baroque rear façade from 1871. Within are 15th-century decorations (see p81).

Altar, Santa Maria presso San Satiro

10 Duomo, Como

Como's cathedral is devoted to Sant'Abbondio, whose life is depicted in the giant gilt altarpiece of 1509–14. Other Renaissance tapestries and paintings, including one by Leonardo's protégé Bernardino Luini, grace the interior (see p113).

Notable Milanese Buildings

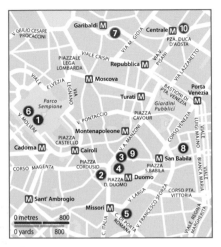

hosted the city's main market. The relief on the façade depicts the 13th-century mayor Oldrado da Tresseno on horseback. Inside, the Salone dei Giudici has its original frescoes (see p81).

3 Palazzo Marino
MAP M3 ■ Piazza della Scala/Piazza S Fedele ■ No public access
Milan's city hall has two distinct façades: a 1553 Mannerist one on Piazza S Fedele, and an 1886–92 Neo-Classical one facing La Scala theatre. The former was built by Galeazzo Alessi (who also designed the lovely main courtyard) in 1558; the latter dates to 1860.

1 Triennale (Palazzo dell'Arte)
On the outskirts of Parco Sempione, the Triennale houses Italy's first Design Museum, with regular design and architecture exhibitions (see p94). The DesignCafé is worth a visit.

2 Palazzo della Ragione
The arcade that occupies the ground level of this Lombard Romanesque palace, built in 1228–33 (the top floor dates from 1771), once

4 Galleria Vittorio Emanuele II
High-class Italian elegance embraced the Industrial Age in such marvels as this four-storey steel-and-glass-canopied arcade, built in 1864–8 by Giuseppe Mengoni. He fell to his death from its scaffolding days before the King arrived to open the galleria and lend it his name (see p83).

Glorious glass-domed shopping arcades of Galleria Vittorio Emanuele II

The 1950s Torre Velasca skyscraper

5 Torre Velasca

When Nathan Rogers, Lodovico Belgioioso and Enrico Peressutti constructed this brick-red, 106-m (348-ft) tower block in 1956–8, they showcased their post-war engineering talents by extending the top nine floors beyond the lower ones on struts, much like an over-sized medieval tower. Unfortunately, the maintenance costs have proved to be horrendous (see p84).

6 Torre Branca

MAP J2 ■ Parco Sempione ■ Open mid-May–mid-Sep: Tue–Sun, mid-Sep–mid-May: Wed, Sat & Sun ■ Adm

This tapering 108-m (354-ft) steel tower was designed by the inter-nationally acclaimed local architect Gio Ponti, and inaugurated in 1933 as part of the fifth edition of the Triennale design exhibition. There's a lift inside to whisk visitors up to the panoramic viewing floor. Formerly called the Torre Littoria, it now takes its name from the Fratelli Branca distillery, which provided funds for the restoration work.

7 Porta Nuova

MAP N1

This area has undergone massive redevelopment to become Milan's most futuristic district. Piazza Gae Aulenti (see p94) is dominated by the Unicredit tower – Italy's tallest, measuring over 230 m (750 ft). The Bosco Verticale (meaning "vertical forest") residential towers and a striking tubular sculpture are among other highlights, while a new public park was scheduled to be inaugurated in autumn 2017.

8 Villa Necchi Campiglio

This perfectly preserved and restored 1930s villa has technology that was revolutionary for its time, including a heated pool and an internal phone system, testimony to the elegant Milanese interwar lifestyle. It houses two important art collections: one of early 20th-century works; the other of 18th-century decorative arts (see p94).

Telamones on Casa degli Omenoni

9 Casa degli Omenoni

Renaissance sculptor Leone Leoni, whose works grace Milan's Duomo and Madrid's El Escorial, built this palazzo in 1565, lining the lower level of the façade with eight giant telamones – columns in the form of a male figure (see p84).

10 Stazione Centrale

MAP S2 ■ Piazza Duca D'Aosta

Milan's massive railway station is often considered a remarkable example of Fascist-era architecture, though its design (of 1912) predates this period and owes more to the Liberty style. Finally completed in 1931, the station is encased in gleaming white Aurisina stone and decorated with reliefs, statues and murals too often overlooked.

🔟 Museums

① Museo Nazionale della Scienza e della Tecnologia – Leonardo da Vinci, Milan

Had Leonardo possessed more technological ambition, we might have had working versions of his helicopters, water screws, Gatling guns, parachutes and siege engines over four centuries ago. As it is, we can make do with the (modern) wooden mock-ups on display at this science and technology museum, alongside instructive exhibits on physics and antique autos and aeroplanes *(see p99)*.

Museo Nazionale della Scienza

② Museo Teatrale alla Scala, Milan

MAP L3–M3 ▪ Largo Ghiringhelli 1 ▪ Open 9am–5:30pm daily ▪ Adm ▪ www.teatroallascala.org

If it has anything to do with the opera in Milan, it's on display here, from costumes worn by Nureyev or Callas to historic instruments, or Verdi's death mask to Toscanini's batons.

③ Castello Sforzesco, Milan

Here you'll find paintings by Bellini and Mantegna, a cycle of 16th-century tapestries, archaeological collections and, its greatest piece, Michelangelo's unfinished *Rondanini Pietà*. Entrance to the castle is free, but there is an entry fee for the Musei Civici within *(see pp20–21)*.

④ Galleria d'Arte Moderna – Villa Belgiojoso Bonaparte, Milan

This fine collection of art, housed in the handsome Villa Belgiojoso Bonaparte *(see p92)*, includes Neo-Classicism and Romanticism works from the beginning of the 20th century plus the Vismara and Grassi collections. Italian 20th-century works can be seen in the Museo del Novecento, which is housed in the Palazzo Reale *(see p81)*.

⑤ Pinacoteca Ambrosiana, Milan

This formidable mix of Old Masters was started by Cardinal Federico Borromeo as an adjunct to the Ambrosiana Library. Famously, the library is home to the *Codex Atlantico*, which contains the lion's share of Leonardo's drawings and sketches – photocopied pages from it are displayed in the Pinacoteca. Elsewhere, you'll find paintings by the likes of Botticelli, Titian and Caravaggio, as well as Raphael's giant preparatory sketch for the *School of Athens (see pp24–5)*.

Leonardo, Pinacoteca Ambrosiana

Interior of the Museo Poldi Pezzoli

6 Museo Poldi Pezzoli, Milan

Poldi Pezzoli's mansion is preserved as a monument to his collections, from Persian tapestries, ancient arms and armour to historic jewellery and, above all, art. In one room alone, there are works by Piero della Francesca, Giovanni Bellini, Mantegna and Botticelli (see p83).

7 Museo del Violino, Cremona

MAP E6 ▪ Piazza Marconi 5 ▪ Open 10am–6pm Tue–Sun ▪ Adm ▪ www.museodelviolino.org

For centuries Cremona has been the world capital of violin-making thanks, among others, to the 17th-century master of the art, Antonio Stradivari. The museum includes fascinating displays – many of which are interactive – on the history, techniques and development of violins, and there are regular performances by soloists on a historic Stradivarius.

8 Pinacoteca di Brera, Milan

This is Lombardy's most important gallery of paintings, displaying works by Mantegna, Giovanni Bellini, Piero della Francesca, Caravaggio, Tintoretto, Veronese, Correggio, Lotto, Carpaccio, Tiepolo, El Greco and Rembrandt (see pp16–19).

9 Galleria dell'Accademia Carrara, Bergamo

Count Giacomo Carrara, a collector of and expert on literature and art, left his collection to his native Bergamo on his death in 1796. Today the gallery houses over 1,800 paintings, including works by Botticelli, Mantegna, Bellini and Raffaello. There is also a significant collection of prints and sketches, sculpture and china. Above all, though, come to admire the emotion-filled Renaissance paintings of Lorenzo Lotto, a Venetian painter who settled in Bergamo in 1513 (see p32).

Museo di Santa Giulia bronze

10 Museo di Santa Giulia, Brescia

Although you will find Romanesque carvings and detached frescoes galore in the cloisters, chapels and chambers of this medieval monastery, the real focus here is on Brescia's great era as a Roman colony, and the archaeological works on display, including a magnificent bronze Winged Victory, are astoundingly beautiful and well preserved (see p49).

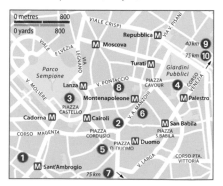

:::TOP 10 Villas and Gardens

Villa Balbianello, perched above the calm waters of Lake Como

① Villa Taranto, Lake Maggiore

MAP A2 ▪ Via Vittorio Veneto, Pallanza ▪ 0323-556-667 ▪ 8:30am–6:30pm daily (Mar: to 5:30pm; Oct & 1 Nov: 9am–4pm) ▪ Closed 2 Nov–mid-Mar ▪ Adm ▪ www.villataranto.it

The villa in the Verbania district (see p108), built in 1875 by Scotsman Neil MacEacharn, is closed to the public, but you can wander the landscaped gardens filled with exotic plants. Rare species include the world's largest water lily at 2 m (6 ft) across and the towering Metasequoia, which was believed extinct for 200 million years until found in China in 1941.

Gardens of the Villa Taranto

② Villa Balbianello, Lake Como

Department store mogul and explorer Guido Monzino gave this 1784 villa and its gorgeous gardens to FAI (the Italian National Trust) in 1988. A museum within chronicles his adventures from Mount Everest to the North Pole. The property topped Como's famous sights list after appearing in Casino Royale and Star Wars: Episode II (see pp52 and 114).

③ Il Vittoriale, Lake Garda

This kitschy Art Nouveau villa was created by poet and adventurer Gabriele d'Annunzio, who once flew a biplane over Vienna in 1918 to prove an invasion was possible, and in 1919 used private troops to take over a border town ceded to Yugoslavia, earning acclaim as a national hero and the enmity of those in power. The villa represents his life, loves and philosophy, which are cheerfully explained by guides. The biplane is on show in an outbuilding (see p126).

④ Villa Monastero, Lake Como

The original structure was not really a monastery, but rather a Cistercian convent founded in 1208. It was disbanded by Charles Borromeo in the 16th century after he heard lascivious stories about its nuns.

It is now owned by a science research centre. You can visit the beautiful terrace of palms, cypresses, roses and magnolias, as well as a greenhouse of citrus trees *(see p113)*.

5 Villa Melzi, Lake Como

The Vice-President of Napoleon's Cisalpine Republic, Francesco Melzi, had this Neo-Classical villa built on Bellagio's southern edge. The villa is off limits, but you can wander the gardens to the water's edge, visit a museum of Etruscan, Egyptian and Roman artifacts and see a mock-Moorish temple that inspired a pair of Liszt piano concertos, written during the composer's stay here *(see p115)*.

6 Villa Serbelloni, Lake Como

The villa's private gardens cover the entire tip of the Bellagio promontory. The guided tours stick mainly to the paths, overlooking the Italianate, English-style and Mediterranean sections. Stendhal described the vista from the top as "sublime and enchanting" – what's more, it is the only spot from which you can see down all three of the arms of Lake Como simultaneously *(see p114)*.

7 Villa Cipressi, Lake Como

MAP C2 ■ Via 4 Novembre, Varenna
The utterly beautiful Villa Cipressi is now an exclusive hotel, and guests can wander its cypress-shaded gardens, blooming with wisteria.

8 Giardino Botanico Hruska, Lake Garda

Over 30 years, Swiss dentist and naturalist Arturo Hruska transformed his single hectare of lake property into a microcosm of Dolomite and Alpine flora. Since 1989, Austrian multimedia artist André Heller has kept it open it to the public *(see p122)*.

Borromeo Palace on the Isola Bella

9 Borromeo Palace, Lake Maggiore

The Borromeo family's 1670 palazzo on the lush Isola Bella is a glimpse into the lifestyle of the wealthiest of Lombard families *(see p30)*.

10 Villa Carlotta, Lake Como

Lake Como is famous for its fabulous villas but, while some gardens are open, few of the buildings themselves can be visited. At Villa Carlotta, however, you can visit both the Baroque villa, with its Neo-Classical statues and Romantic paintings, and the extensive, lush gardens *(see p114)*.

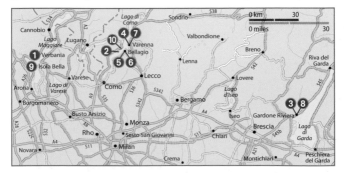

🔟 Small Towns and Villages

View of Cremona from its Torrazzo

1 Cremona
MAP E6 ■ Tourist info: Piazza del Comune 5 ■ www.turismo cremona.it

Cremona's attractive medieval centre is dominated by the Torrazzo bell tower, the city's symbol; views from the top are stunning. Nearby, the Museo del Violino (see p45) tells the story of Cremona's enduring claim to fame, violin making.

2 Borghetto sul Mincio
MAP C5 ■ Tourist info: Piazza Carlo Alberto 44, Valeggio sul Mincio ■ www.valeggio.com

This exquisitely beautiful village, just 20 minutes south of Lake Garda, features a series of watermills and an imposing 14th century bridge.

Pretty Borghetto sul Mincio

3 Lodi
MAP D5 ■ Tourist info: Piazza Broletto 4 ■ 0371-409-238 ■ www.turismolodi.it

Medieval Lodi is celebrated for its Duomo and octagonal church of the Incoronata. The latter is slathered with frescoes, gilded stuccoes and fine paintings by Il Bergognone.

4 Vigevano
MAP B5 ■ Tourist info: Via Ruga 44 ■ 0381-690-269

Lodovico Sforza (see p39) was born in the castle that dominates this town of silk and shoe factories. The arcaded Piazza Ducale is by Bramante; the Baroque Duomo was built in 1680.

Arcaded Piazza Ducale in Vigevano

5 Pavia
MAP C6 ■ Tourist info: Via del Comune 18 (Piazza della Vittoria) ■ 0382-07-9943 ■ www.visitpavia.com

The Dark Ages capital of Northern Italy retains its historic centre. As well as the Certosa (see p41), other important churches include the Duomo, of which Leonardo was one architect. There's also a Renaissance bridge and a 14th-century castle with paintings by Bellini and Tiepolo.

6 Brunate
MAP C3 ■ www.funicolare como.it

The funicular from Como leads up to this charming hillside village, which has stunning views over the city and lake, and a mix of Liberty villas and mountain architecture. There are excellent walking trails from here.

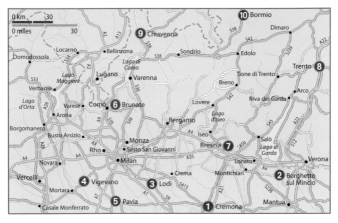

7 Brescia
MAP F4 ■ Tourist info:
Piazzale Stazione ■ 030-837-8559
■ www.provincia.brescia.it

Brescia has a fine medieval and
Renaissance centre, with traces of
its time as a Roman colony. The San
Salvatore e Santa Giulia monastery
displays prehistoric, Roman and
medieval artifacts, and the art gallery
has works by Raphael and Tintoretto.

8 Trento
MAP H2 ■ Tourist info: Piazza
Dante 24 ■ www.discovertrento.it

Given its Alpine location and historic
centre with sights from every era
from ancient Roman times onwards,
Trento is a joy to explore. There's
also an innovative science museum.

9 Chiavenna
MAP D1 ■ Tourist info: Piazza
Caduti della Libertà ■ 0343-374-85
■ www.valchiavenna.com

Set in an Alpine valley, Chiavenna
is littered with *crotti* – caverns used
to cure meats and cheeses – some
of which have been converted into
osterie. An old stone quarry above
town is home to a botanical park,
and the Parco Marmitte dei Giganti
contains prehistoric carvings.

10 Bormio
Tourist info: Via Roma 131b
■ 0342-903-300 ■ www.valtellina.it

This year-round skiing village high in
the Valtellina is equal parts upmarket
resort and medieval village. It's also
a gateway to a park full of glaciers,
peaks, trails and lovely Alpine vistas.

Trento's medieval cathedral square

🔟 Lombard Experiences

Cruising on Lake Como

1 A Cruise on Lake Como
The loveliest of the Italian lakes *(see pp112–19)* is best enjoyed from the waters. From this vantage point, devoid of traffic jams, you can see the glorious gardens and villas lining its banks (from the road, all you may see is a high wall).

2 Snacking on a Café Crawl
Between about 6pm and 9pm, many Milanese bars and cafés have Happy Hour, when a cocktail costs between €7 and €15 and includes a buffet spread with several courses (meat, fish or pasta). You can easily make a decent early dinner out of it.

3 A Night at the Opera
At Italy's premier opera house, La Scala, you can enjoy one of the world's best companies in a wondrous 18th-century setting. Inside there is a museum, and guided tours of the theatre are available *(see p82)*.

4 A Violin Concert in Cremona
In the city where Nicolò Amati honed his craft and passed his skills on to Stradivari, they take their violins seriously. Virtuosos from around the globe come to numerous festivals, concert seasons and trade fairs just for the chance to bow a few sonatas on the city's magnificent collection of original Strads *(see pp45 and 48)*.

5 Sports on Lake Garda
The northern end of Lake Garda is buffeted by strong winds blowing down from the Sarca Valley in the north in the morning (the *sover*) and south up the lake in the afternoon (the *ora*). Together, they make for some of the best wind-surfing and sailing conditions on any lake in Western Europe, and all summer long watersports fans flock from far and wide to Riva and its neighbour Torbole to thrash the waves *(see p124)*.

6 A Milanese Shopping Spree
Milan is one of the world capitals of high fashion, home to dozens of top designer names *(see pp72–3)* in its famed Quadrilatero d'Oro – "Golden Rectangle" – of streets *(see p71)*. Add in designer household objects, chic leather goods, Como silk, fine wines and foods, and Milan becomes a shopper's paradise.

Production of Puccini's *Madama Butterfly* at La Scala opera house

7 An Evening on the Navigli

Milan's southern district of canals and warehouses has been converted to a vibrant and bustling evening area of restaurants, pizzerias, bars, pubs and funky shops *(see pp28–9)*.

8 Exploring the Roof of Milan's Duomo

You can wander freely amongst the forest of Gothic carving adorning the rooftop of Milan's cathedral, and onto the peaked roof of the nave for fine views across the city *(see p14)*.

Exploring the Duomo's rooftop

9 Hill Walking near the Lakes

Local tourist offices can often supply maps of mountain trails. Pick a point of interest as a goal: a ruined castle (Arco on Garda, Varenna on Como), church (Madonna del Sasso above Locarno on Maggiore, San Pietro above Civate on Como), mountain stream (Fiumelatte by Varenna, Cascata del Varone above Riva del Garda), or prehistoric rock carvings.

10 San Siro Stadium

MAP R2 ▪ Piazzale Angelo Moratti ▪ Open 9:30am–6pm daily (except match days) ▪ Adm ▪ www.sansiro.net

Milan's football stadium is Italy's largest and hosts the home games of two of the country's top teams, AC Milan and Inter Milan. Watching a match here is a memorable experience, while the stadium tour and museum offer a fascinating behind-the-scenes glimpse into the clubs.

TOP 10 LAKESIDE ATTRACTIONS

Charming Varenna on Lake Como

1 Varenna, Lake Como
This attractive, authentic village has a waterfront promenade, villas, gardens, churches and a half-ruined castle *(see p117)*.

2 Isole Borromee, Lake Maggiore
A trio of islets off Stresa – two clad in gardens and palaces, the third with a quaint fishing village *(see pp30–31)*.

3 Santa Caterina del Sasso, Lake Maggiore
A medieval church in a cliff face, just above the water's edge *(see p108)*.

4 Rocca di Angera, Lake Maggiore
This 8th-century Lombard fortress dominates the headland *(see p107)*.

5 Bellagio, Lake Como
Perhaps the loveliest town on any of the lakes, with an arcaded harbour, steep alleyways, elegant villas and sumptuous gardens *(see p117)*.

6 Como's Duomo, Lake Como
The exterior of the cathedral is a feast of statues and bas-reliefs *(see p113)*.

7 Villa Carlotta, Lake Como
Visitors can enter this fabulous, art-filled villa, as well as wander round its botanical gardens *(see p114)*.

8 Il Vittoriale, Lake Garda
An over-the-top Art Nouveau villa owned by adventurer and poet Gabriele d'Annuzio *(see p126)*.

9 Sirmione, Lake Garda
A picture-perfect town set on a narrow peninsula, with a dramatic castle, and a ruined Roman villa *(see pp121 & 122)*.

10 Giardino Botanico Hruska, Lake Garda
A labour of love by a Swiss dentist, these gardens offer visitors a vista of the Alps amid the lakes *(see p122)*.

🔟 Books and Films Set in Lombardy

1 I Promessi Sposi (The Betrothed)

Written in the 1800s, Alessandro Manzoni's novel is a window into Lombard life in the 1600s, set in Milan and Manzoni's Lake Como home town of Lecco during Spanish rule. It is required reading for all Italian schoolchildren and has been translated into many languages.

Manzoni, author of *The Betrothed*

2 A Month by the Lake

This gentle romantic comedy, based on a short story by H E Bates, is set in 1937 on the shores of Lake Como. Vanessa Redgrave, Edward Fox and Uma Thurman head up the cast of the 1995 movie by John Irvin. Much of it was filmed in and around Varenna and Bellagio *(see p117)*.

3 Casino Royale

The beautiful grounds of Villa Balbianello on Lake Como *(see p114)* featured in this James Bond film in 2006. Fans can also check out the famous Villa Gaeta, the location for the last scene in the movie. This private house, in Art Nouveau style, lies between Menaggio and Dongo, and is best seen from the ferry boat.

4 Theorem

Pier Paolo Pasolini's usual mix of sex, homosexuality and a communist critique on the emptiness of bourgeois life defines this 1968 film. Enigmatic stranger Terence Stamp raises the libidos of a Milanese family, then further stirs up their lives by disappearing.

5 Miracle in Milan

Vittorio de Sica's 1951 fable of a magical dove that grants wishes to the inhabitants of a Milan slum uses an early version of "special effects", bridging the popular Neo-Realistic style of Italy's post war cinema with the era of magical realism in Italian film-making that Fellini would make famous.

6 A Traveller in Italy

H V Morton who, in his youth, scooped the story of Tutankhamun's tomb discovery in the 1920s, became one of the 20th-century's finest, if little-known, travel writers. His 1950s journey through Italy is an erudite combination of travelogue, history and wonderful prose, much of it surprisingly undated.

7 The Spider's Stratagem

Before gaining international fame, Bernardo Bertolucci made this 1969 story of a dysfunctional family haunted by the Fascist past. He set this psychological drama in the quirky town of Sabbioneta.

Scene from *The Spider's Stratagem*

Monica Vitti in Antonioni's *La Notte*

8 La Notte

Film director Michelangelo Antonioni sets the slow death of affection between a couple, played by Marcello Mastroianni and Jeanne Moreau, against a backdrop of rapidly industralizing Milan in 1960.

1957 film of *A Farewell to Arms*

9 A Farewell to Arms

Ernest Hemingway's World War I novel (written in 1929) tells the story of a wounded American soldier reuniting with his love in Stresa on Lake Maggiore. They stay at the Grand Hôtel des Iles Borromées, where Hemingway himself often stayed, then flee by boat across the lake to Swiss Locarno.

10 Twilight in Italy

The first place D H Lawrence and his lover Frieda settled during their European travels was on Lake Garda, during the winter of 1912–13. In 1916 he compiled this travelogue.

TOP 10 LA SCALA PREMIERES

1 L'Europa Riconosciuta (1778)
Antonio Salieri's bellicose but light-hearted opera was first performed at La Scala on 3 August 1778.

2 La Pietra del Paragone (1812)
Rossini's work signalled La Scala's shift from comic opera and Neo-Classical works to Romantic melodrama.

3 Chiara e Serafina (1822)
The first of many fun-loving Donizetti premieres was this lively piratical tale.

4 Norma (1831)
Of Bellini's three La Scala premieres, the most famous is Norma, a Druid-Roman love triangle that ends badly.

5 Nabucco (1842)
Verdi would become La Scala's greatest home-grown composer, but he suffered two flops before this hit.

6 Mefistofele (1868)
Boito's first great success led to a collaboration with Verdi that produced Otello in 1887 and Falstaff in 1893.

7 Aïda (1872)
After a long absence from La Scala, Verdi offered this Egyptian melodrama.

8 Madama Butterfly (1904)
Puccini's tale of enduring love between a Japanese geisha and an American soldier was received badly at first.

9 Turandot (1926)
Over a year after his death, Puccini's final and unfinished opera premiered at La Scala, conducted by Toscanini.

10 The Rake's Progress (1951)
Under Toscanini's direction, La Scala started opening up to foreign works, including this Stravinsky classic.

Interior of La Scala opera house

🔟 Artists Working in Lombardy

Fresco of the Court of Gonzaga, by Mantegna, in Mantua

1 Andrea Mantegna (1431–1506)

Mantegna's classical mode of High Renaissance painting differed from, but was as beautiful as, that of his brother-in-law Giovanni Bellini. In 1460 he became court painter to the Gonzagas of Mantua, where he left masterful frescoes on the walls of the Palazzo Ducale *(see pp34–5)*. Milan's Pinacoteca di Brera houses his masterpiece, *Dead Christ (see p17)*.

2 Bramante (1444–1514)

The great architect of the High Renaissance travelled from Urbino to Rome, leaving churches in his wake, and even doing a stint as chief architect of St Peter's in Rome.

Sketches by Leonardo da Vinci

3 Leonardo da Vinci (1452–1519)

The ultimate Renaissance Man was a genius painter, inventor and scientist. His inventions – which included helicopters, machine guns and water systems – were centuries ahead of their time but mostly confined to sketches, though working models have been built at Milan's technical museum *(see pp44 & 99)*.

4 Bernardino Luini (1475–1532)

This apprentice of Leonardo was so taken with his master's talents that he spent his life painting in the style of Leonardo without ever really developing one of his own.

5 Il Bergognone (1480–1523)

With the Renaissance going on all around him, Il Bergognone remained firmly a late Gothic artist, painting lovely but staid devotional works rooted in the style of his Milanese predecessor Vincenzo Foppa.

6 Giulio Romano (1499–1546)

Raphael's protégé helped finish his master's commissions after his death, but his fame as a frescoist was soon eclipsed by his architectural technique. Both came to the attention of the Gonzagas in Mantua, who commissioned from him the Palazzo Te *(see p35)* and other buildings. Only failing health kept him from returning to Rome to become chief architect of St Peter's.

7 Giuseppe Arcimboldo (1527–93)

This Milanese Mannerist may have been a gimmick artist, but he was very good at it. He churned out many allegorical "portraits" that are in fact collages: of flowers, fruit, weapons, fish, animals or even flames.

Collage portrait by Arcimboldo

8 Caravaggio (1571–1609/10)

The Baroque master, who influenced an entire generation, used peasant models and a technique of heavy chiaroscuro, playing harsh light off deep black shadows to create dramatic scenes with brilliant realism.

9 Francesco Hayez (1707–76)

Born in Venice, Hayez moved to Rome – where he mixed with Ingres and Canova – then Milan, balancing his painting between the Romantic and Neo-Classical ideals of the age. He eventually became director of the Pinacoteca di Brera.

10 Umberto Boccioni (1882–1916)

This leading Futurist was born in the south but soon moved to Milan. His failed journalism career served him in writing treatises on Futurism, and his paintings and sculptures were among the most admired of his era.

TOP 10 ARTISTIC ERAS IN LOMBARDY

1 Ancient
From prehistoric rock etchings dating back to the 12th century BC to Roman villas of the 5th century AD.

2 Lombard
Lombard buildings from the 5th to 10th centuries have triangular façades, blind arcades and ribbed vaulting.

3 Romanesque
Architectural style in the 11th and 12th centuries defined by rounded arches and crude, expressive carvings.

4 Gothic
Pointed arches and flying buttresses allowed ceilings to soar in the 13th and 14th centuries. Painting became more expressive and realistic.

5 Renaissance
Classical architecture and elegant painting, with delicate colours and new techniques such as perspective (in the 15th–16th centuries).

6 Baroque
Similar to the Renaissance but with profuse decor; big in the 17th century, but then spiralled into overwrought Rococo in the 18th century.

7 Neo-Classical
Late 18th- to early 19th century quest for the soul of the ancients; austere.

8 Romantic
A 19th-century return to the Gothic age and overwrought decor.

9 Liberty
The Italian Art Nouveau of the early 20th century delighted in asymmetrical organic curves.

10 Futurist
Italy's Cubism was obsessed with the fast, modern technological world of the early 20th century.

Ancient rock art near Brescia

Sports and Activities

1 Cycling
AWS, Milan: www.awsbici.com
■ Xtreme Malcesine, Lake Garda:
www.xtrememalcesine.com

Cycle the canalside paths of Navigli
(see p28), hit the mountain-biking
trails of Monte Baldo above Lake
Garda (see p124) or explore the
Franciacorta wine area using two-
wheeled transport (see p132).

2 Golf
Golf Club Milano: www.golf
clubmilano.com ■ Menaggio &
Cadenabbia Golf Club: www.
menaggio.org

The 27-hole Milan Golf Club is one
of the nation's best, and there's a
high concentration of clubs at Lake
Garda (see p124). The Menaggio &
Cadenabbia club at Lake Como is
also excellent, as is the Franciacorta
club near Lake Iseo (see p132).

3 Climbing
Arco, Lake Garda: www.move.
net; www.arcowall.com ■ Lake Como:
www.lakecomoadventures.com

Milan has several indoor climbing
walls, but for the real thing Arco,
at the northern end of Lake Garda,
has plenty of bolted climbing routes
(see p124). Lake Como Adventures
runs courses for different abilities
at various locations.

Tackling a cliff above Lake Como

Windsurfing on Lake Garda

4 Windsurfing and Kitesurfing
Surf Segnana, Torbole: www.
surfsegnana.it ■ Europa Surf & Sail,
Malcesine: www.europasurfandsail.
com ■ La Darsena, Lake Maggiore:
www.ladarsenawindsurf.com

Torbole, at the northern end of Lake
Garda (see p124), is one of Europe's
premier windsurfing locations and
there are good winds at Malcesine
too. The northern tips of Lake Como
(see p116) and Lake Maggiore are
also favourite spots and equipment
hire and courses are available at
various places around the lakes.

5 Swimming
Piscina Solari: Via Montevideo
20, Milan

Milan's Idroscalo (see p61) has
beaches and open-air swimming
pools, ideal for a refreshing dip on a
hot summer's day, while year-round
indoor pools include Piscina Solari.
And, of course, the cool, clear waters
of the lakes are highly inviting.

6 Ice-Skating
Agorà: Via dei Ciclamini 23;
www.stadioghiaccio.it

The largest indoor ice-rink in Milan,
Agorà is southwest of the centre and
has regular public sessions. Open-
air ice-rinks pop up over Christmas,
including one in futuristic Piazza Gae
Aulenti (see p94) and another on
Como's lakeside Piazza Cavour.

7 Walking

Walking tours of Milan include free half-day tours (see p74), while at the lakes there are classic routes such as the Antica Strada Valeriana at Lake Iseo (see p132) and the Via Regina on the west coast of Lake Como.

8 Skiing

Fly Ski Shuttle: www. flyskishuttle.com ■ **Cable-car Mottarone:** www.stresa-mottarone.it
Thanks to Milan's position near the Alps, a vast range of ski resorts are within easy reach and there's a good shuttle service from the airports. The season starts on 7 December to coincide with the festival of the city's patron, Sant'Ambrogio. Cable-cars take skiers up to to Monte Baldo from Lake Garda (see p124) and to Mottarone from Lake Maggiore.

Skiers on Monte Baldo

9 Boats

Kayaking is a fantastic way to explore the lakes; equipment hire is widely available. The lake ferry companies run cruises and there are lots of small-scale private boat tours.

10 Spas

QC Terme Milano: Piazza Medaglie d'Oro; wwww.qcterme.com ■ **Aquaria, Sirmione:** www.termedi sirmione.com
Time out at one of Milan's many spas is the perfect way to relax. QC Terme, for example, is elegantly luxurious, and includes a bio-spa within a historic tram. Sirmione on Lake Garda is particularly good for spas thanks to the natural thermal water bubbling up at 69° C (156° F).

TOP 10 SPECTATOR SPORTS

Vintage cars in the Mille Miglia

1 Car Racing
www.1000miglia.it
The Mille Miglia vintage car race goes from Brescia to Rome and back.

2 Football
AC Milan and Internazionale (also known as Inter) both play at the city's magnificent San Siro stadium (see p51).

3 Basketball
www.olimpiamilano.com
Italians love basketball; Olimpia Milano is one of the country's top teams.

4 Motorsports
www.monzanet.it
Events held at the Monza track include the Formula One Italian Grand Prix.

5 Horse racing
www.ippodromitrenno.it
Milan's main racecourse is northwest of the city centre, next to San Siro.

6 Ice hockey
www.hockeymilano.it
Hockey Milano Rossoblu is the local team, playing in the top league.

7 Rugby
asr.imginternet.it
The local top-league club is AS Rugby Milano; Italy is part of the Six Nations.

7 Volleyball
www.powervolleymilano.it
■ www.verovolley.com
Milan's top-league teams are Milano Power and Milano Vero Volley.

8 American Football
www.rhinos.it ■ www.seamen.it
The city's two top teams in Milan are the Rhinos and the Seamen.

9 Cycling
www.giroditalia.it
The first edition of the Giro d'Italia race set off from Milan in 1909 and the city often hosts the final stage.

Off the Beaten Track

1 Parco Agricolo Sud di Milano

MAP C3 ■ www.parcoagricolosud milano.it ■ Rice-growing area: www. parcodellerisaie.it

This vast area of agricultural and natural parkland surrounds two-thirds of the city to the south, east and west, and includes the major rice-growing area towards Pavia. Its villages, wildlife reserves and farmsteads (cascine), many with restaurants, are popular among the Milanese for a day out.

2 Monza and Brianza

MAP C4 ■ Tourist Board Monza: www.turismo.monza.it ■ Villa Reale: www.reggiadimonza.it ■ Brianza villas: www.villeaperte.info

Monza is at the heart of the Brianza area. The vast parkland surrounding the majestic Villa Reale contains Monza's famous racetrack, Milan Golf Club (see p56), and an open-air swimming pool. Brianza has several grand villas and churches.

Monza's cathedral and bell tower

3 Triangolo Lariano

MAP C3

Lakes Pusiano and Annone are two of a series of peaceful minor lakes in this stretch of land between Como and Lecco. Lake Annone is divided almost in two by a narrow peninsula, and is overlooked by the San Pietro al Monte monastery (see p118).

Abbazia di Chiaravalle's cloisters

4 Abbazia di Chiaravalle

MAP S3 ■ Open Tue–Sun ■ www.monasterochiaravalle.it

The most striking of the series of working abbeys to the south of Milan, this medieval structure has an unusual octagonal bell tower (Ciribiciaccola in the local dialect), an interesting frescoed interior, with some painted by Bernardino Luini, attractive cloisters and a historic mill. Produce from the on-site farm and from other nearby farms is sold.

5 Foraging in Desio

MAP C4 ■ Wood-ing: www. wood-ing.org

The Wood-ing Wild Food Lab, which is based at Desio, just north of Milan, organizes enjoyable and eye-opening half-day foraging courses in a range of languages. They also run longer trips further afield, intensive professional courses for chefs and tasting evenings with high-quality dishes made from a wide range of unexpected natural produce, including tree bark.

6 Trezzo sull'Adda

MAP D4 ■ Trezzo sull'Adda Tourist Board: www.prolocotrezzo. com ■ River-boats: www.navigare inlombardia.it

This charming town stands on the banks of the Adda at a double bend in the river – boat trips run on summer weekends. Trezzo can be reached from Milan via the cycle-path from Cascina dei Pomi along the Martesana canal, and is dominated by the ruins of the 14th-century Castello Visconteo.

7 **Valle Intelvi**

This mountain valley links Lake Lugano and Lake Como. There are plenty of excellent walking opportunities for all abilities and, at Schignano, an easy woodland footpath, the Sentiero delle Espressioni, passes a series of wooden sculptures. Monte Sighignola, which rises 1,300 m (4,265 ft), has a panoramic terrace just below the summit, known as the Balcony of Italy, with stunning views across the Alps (see p118).

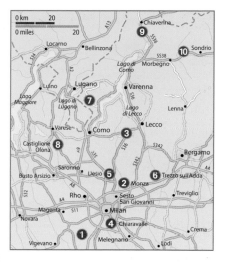

8 **Castiglione Olona**

MAP B3 ■ Castiglione Olona: www.prolococastiglioneolona.it ■ Castelseprio: www.castelseprio.net

This medieval village on the banks of the River Olona retains its attractive centre thanks largely to intervention by 14th-century Cardinal Branda Castiglioni. His bedroom within the Palazzo Branda Castiglioni has some exquisite frescoes, as does the chapel. Nearby, the fine monastic complex of Torba was originally a Roman fortress.

9 **Valchiavenna**

MAP D1 ■ Valchiavenna Tourist Board: www.valchiavenna.com

Pretty and historic Chiavenna is the main centre of the mountainous Valchiavenna area just

north of Lake Como, while nearby Madesimo is a lively ski resort in winter. The footpaths of the Marmitte dei Giganti park near Chiavenna (see p118) take walkers past a series of unusual rock formations, including ice-polished channels, shafts and potholes, and there is a wealth of figurative and geometric ancient rock carvings to be seen.

10 **Valtellina**

Valtellina is a stunning mountain area with excellent sports facilities, charming historic villages such as Bormio, Teglio and Tirano, and a notable food and wine culture. The landscape is scattered with terraces where Nebbiolo grapes for the characterful Valtellina red wines, are grown. Local speciality dishes include *pizzoccheri*, hearty buckwheat ribbons (see p118).

The lake at Valchiavenna

📊 **Children's Attractions**

Gardaland's bright and kid-friendly attractions

① MUBA – Museo dei Bambini

MAP N4 ▪ Via Besana 12, Milan ▪ 02-4398-0402 ▪ Open 9:30am–6pm Tue–Sun ▪ Adm ▪ www.muba.it

In the centre of a public park, and designed specifically for children, this museum offers a lively calendar of activities for 1–12-year-olds.

② The Best Science Museum in Italy

Milan's Museo Nazionale della Scienza e della Tecnologia has the usual impressive, interactive displays of any major science museum – plus Leonardo. Here, full-scale models of his ahead-of-their-time inventions (including the helicopter – on paper, anyway) bring his astonishing ideas to life *(see p99)*.

Studying a Leonardo machine

③ Gardaland

Italy's top theme park, on the southeastern banks of Lake Garda, is not quite Disneyland, but it does have roller coasters, a jungle safari, reconstructions of the Pyramids and a thrilling water park. The facilities are good, including a range of refreshments, themed shops and souvenir photos *(see p123)*.

④ Lakeside Castles

You can relive the Middle Ages by exploring Lombardy's castles, scrambling up watchtowers and patrolling the ramparts like a soldier of old. At Castello Sforzesco in Milan *(see pp20–21)*, regular tours take you up onto the battlements. Those on the lakes can be more atmospheric. The best fortresses are at Varenna *(see p117)*, Arco *(see p123)*, Malcesine *(see p125)* and Sirmione *(see p122)*.

⑤ Alpyland

MAP A3 ▪ Località Mottarone, Stresa ▪ Adm ▪ www.alpyland.com

Zipping down the 1200-m (3,937-ft) track on the Alpine Coaster, a bobsled rollercoaster at the top of Mount Mottarone (cable-car from Stresa) is an exhilarating experience. The two-seater bobsleds have an individual braking system, and the location guarantees stunning views.

6 Idroscalo

MAP T2 ▪ Open 8am–9pm daily (Nov–Mar: to 5pm) ▪ Adm ▪ www.idroscalo.info

This large artificial lake near Linate airport offers beaches and pools, bicycle hire, a children's play park and watersports, as well as a range of cafés and picnic sites.

7 Prada Accademia dei Bambini

MAP S2 ▪ Largo Iscaro 2, Milan ▪ Open 11am–5pm Sat & Sun ▪ www.fondazioneprada.org

At the Prada Children's Academy, top experts from a variety of disciplines, including the arts and sciences, lead fun, free weekly workshops that need to be booked in advance.

8 Gelato Breaks

Italy's gelato puts all other ice creams to shame. There are dozens of classic parlours around Milan – look out for natural colours, as well as for the sign *"produzione propria"*, indicating that it's homemade.

Luscious Italian ice cream

9 Cycling in Mantua

The city of Mantua is flat, virtually surrounded by lakes and plains that stretch up and down the Mincio River, all of it begging to be explored on two wheels *(see pp34–5)*.

10 Puppet Shows

MAP P5 ▪ Teatro Silvestrianum, Via Andrea Maffei 19, Milan ▪ 02-5521-1300 ▪ Oct–Apr ▪ www.teatrocolla.org

Master puppeteers Cosetta and Gianni Colla keep Italy's rich tradition of puppetry alive and updated.

TOP 10 MILAN CITY PARKS

Park Lambro, the city's largest

1 Parco Lambro
MAP C4 ▪ Via Feltre
This large country-park has play areas and a skateboard park.

2 Parco di Porta Nuova
MAP M1 ▪ Via Gaetano de' Castillia
The city's newest park has a so-called library of trees made up of mini-forests.

3 Parco Sempione
MAP J1 ▪ Piazza Sempione
This substantial 19th century park has a children's play area, a lake and cafés.

4 Giardino Indro Montanelli
MAP N1–P1 ▪ Corso Venezia
An 18th-century public park. A plant market/exhibition is held each May.

5 Boscoincittà
MAP C4 ▪ Via Novara
A haven of woodland, streams and lakes, green areas and cycle paths.

6 Giardini della Guastalla
MAP N5 ▪ Via Francesco Sforza
Milan's oldest park, dating from 1555, has a Baroque fish pond with lotuses.

7 Parco Solari
MAP J5 ▪ Via Solari
A pleasant city park with a swimming pool, near the Navigli canal district.

8 Giardini della Villa Belgiojoso Bonaparte
MAP N2 ▪ Via Palestro
A park reserved for children; adults can only enter if accompanied by one.

9 Giardino Perego
MAP M2 ▪ Via dei Giardini
An appealing little park with lots of trees and a children's play area.

10 Parco Papa Giovanni Paolo II
MAP L5 ▪ Via Vetere
A pleasant park set in a remarkable position between the Sant'Eustorgio and San Lorenzo basilicas.

TOP10 Entertainment Venues in Milan

Teatro degli Arcimboldi dancers

③ Auditorium di Milano
MAP R2 ■ Via S Gottardo 39
■ www.laverdi.org

Since 1999, the "Giuseppe Verdi" Symphony Orchestra of Milan has played in this re-invented 1930s cinema, which stood derelict for decades after World War II. The orchestra, under Conductor Riccardo Chailly and musical director Xian Zhang, has a repertoire ranging from Bach to 19th-century symphonic music and contemporary pieces.

④ Lime Light
This is high-tech nightclubbing, with TV screens, Internet feeds, concerts broadcast live and a magnetic card that keeps track of your tab (you pay when you leave). The music ranges from modern pop and hip-hop to 1960s and 1970s revival – the owners are a group of Serie A footballers, who are often seen here when not on the field (see p102).

① Teatro degli Arcimboldi
MAP S1 ■ Viale dell'Innovazione 20 ■ www.teatroarcimboldi.it

Opened in 2002 as an alternative to La Scala while the latter was undergoing restoration work, this striking theatre in the redeveloped Bicocca district has a capacity of over 2,300, making it Europe's second largest.

② La Scala
Housed in a glorious 18th-century theatre, this is one of the world's top opera companies, where Verdi was house composer, Callas graced the stage and costumes are designed by top fashion names. The season runs from December to May, so book well in advance (see p82).

⑤ Alcatraz
Located on a street that features a number of hip nightspots, Milan's largest club is housed in a converted industrial space and hosts live music concerts, events and parties. The action begins around 11pm and goes on until about 3am.

Grand operatic performance taking place on the stage of La Scala

art and cultural events. With a maximum capacity of almost 3,000, it attracts well-known stars from the international music scene, from Sting to Rag'n'Bone Man.

8 Blue Note

The first European outpost of the famed New York jazz club serves up dinner and top-line performers from Tuesday to Saturday, and a jazz brunch on Sundays. The line-up is wide-ranging. Past acts have ranged from Bill Evans and Suzanne Vega to the London Community Gospel Choir. Booking is essential (see p96).

9 Hollywood

This stalwart from the 1980s still offers you the best chance in all of Milan to spot a genuine international supermodel, making Corso Como one of the city's most fashionable streets. Though a perfectly standard discotheque from 1986, glitzy Hollywood continues to draw the most beautiful people in town, so dress to impress (see p96).

There is often live music during the week and dancing every Saturday and Sunday, with three rooms playing different types of music (see p96).

6 Old Fashion Cafe
MAP J2 ▪ Viale E. Alemagna 6
▪ 02-805-6231 ▪ www.oldfashion.it

This veteran of the Milan nightlife scene remains popular, judging by the crowds hanging around outside waiting to get past the velvet rope. Situated in the Palazzo dell'Arte in Parco Sempione, it has an elegant restaurant and a cosy lounge, both with dance floors. In summer the crowd spills out into the large garden.

7 Fabrique
MAP S2 ▪ Via Fantoli 9 ▪ 02-5801-8197 ▪ www.fabriquemilano.it

Occupying the former premises of a record warehouse, Fabrique is one of Milan's newest and most successful venues, hosting regular live concerts, club evenings and plenty of other events as well, including fashion,

Live music at Magazzini Generali

10 Magazzini Generali
MAP R2 ▪ Via Pietrasanta 14
▪ www.magazzinigenerali.org

Cavernous Magazzini Generali has an auditorium that seats 1,000 for live acts, and it can become a huge disco. It also has a gallery for exhibitions, live poetry readings and more.

TOP 10 Culinary Highlights of Lombardy

Pan-fried Cotoletta alla Milanese

1 Cotoletta alla Milanese

For proof that the Lombards are Germanic at heart, look no further than Milan's archetypal dish, a breaded veal cutlet which is similar to Wiener schnitzel.

2 Ossobuco

Veal chops are cut across the shin bone, lightly fried, then slow-cooked in wine and tomatoes, and served with lemon-parsley-garlic gremolata tossed on top. Proper *ossobuco* is served on the bone (its very name means "bone-hole"): digging out the rich marrow is considered an integral part of enjoying the dish.

3 Strangolapreti

These little spinach and ricotta balls are called "priest-stranglers" because they are deemed so rich they'd choke a poor prelate's simple palate. Traditionally served simply with butter and grated parmesan.

4 Tortelli di Zucca

Mantua specializes in this slightly sweet first course, stuffing pockets of fresh pasta with a rich pumpkin paste. It's usually topped with a simple butter and sage sauce.

5 Cheeses

Lombardy is the land of Italy's king of blue-veined cheeses, gorgonzola, and its lesser-known cousin taleggio (no mould, just strongly odoured goodness). It is also home to Parmesan cheese: Grana Padano, Parmigiano Reggiano and Grana Lodigiano. On the milder end of the scale are the popular Bel Paese and spreadable, creamy mascarpone.

6 Lake Fish

Several fish favourites are plucked daily from Lombardy's lakes. The best include *persico* (perch), *lavarello* (a whitefish), *trota* (trout), *luccio* (pike), *coregone* (another whitefish) and *tinca* (tench).

7 Panettone

All across Italy at Christmas people snap up boxes of this traditional Lombard cake, though locals enjoy it year-round. It is quite dry, and studded with fruit and candied peel.

Light, fruity panettone

8 Cassoeûla

Somewhere between a soup and a stew, this Milanese dish throws sausage and chunks of pork into a thick cabbage broth, with polenta on the side. It'll stick to your ribs (and clog your arteries).

Cassoeûla

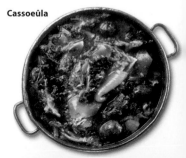

Soft polenta with a savoury topping

9 Polenta

Northern Italy's cornmeal side dish can be prepared in a wide range of ways, from a creamy, molten mass rich with butter and cheese to a set paste which is sliced and fried until crisp and golden. Modern cooks also use it as a gluten-free alternative in baking, or in place of breadcrumbs for coating food to be fried.

Saffron-hued risotto alla Milanese

10 Risotto alla Milanese

If you order risotto in Italy, you usually have to wait at least 20 minutes, as the cook must constantly stir the rice until it reaches the perfect texture. It is time-consuming to make in small batches, so some restaurants will prepare it only for two or more people. In Milan, they often tinge their risotto bright yellow with saffron, and may throw in some seasonal vegetables. In Mantua, they usually spice it up with sausage.

TOP 10 WINES

1 Bardolino
This wine is a light, balanced red from Lake Garda's Veneto shore.

2 Valtellina
This meaty red from the hills around Lake Como is intensely aromatic and powerful: one type is named "Inferno".

3 Franciacorta
Italy's answer to champagne. This superior sparkling wine is usually made with Chardonnay, Pinot Noir and Pinot Bianco grapes.

4 Oltrepò Pavese
Also slightly fizzy, lighter and tangier than Lambrusco. The Garda region also produces familiar varietals.

5 Garda Bresciano
A collection of wines from the lower reaches of Lake Garda, including Gropello and the rounder Chiaretto from the Mincio valley.

6 San Martino della Battaglia
A tart white made from Tocai grapes of Friuli; there's also a velvety, fortified dessert liqueur version.

7 Lugana
This balanced white is made from Trebbiano grapes on the southern shores of Lake Garda.

8 San Colombano
Milan's own red wine is primarily significant for achieving the DOC level of status despite being grown on the outskirts of an industrial city.

9 Grappa
Italy's own brand of firewater is a *digestivo* ("digestive" liqueur) which is distilled from the leftovers of the grape-squeezing process.

10 Lambrusco
Thick, dark, fizzy red from Mantua. Cheap but delicious; great with pizza.

Sparkling, sweet Lambrusco

Restaurants

1 Villa Fiordaliso, Lake Garda

Beyond the historic Liberty-style villa (now a hotel) where D'Annunzio lived and Mussolini's mistress spent her final days, the tables are set about a shaded terrace lapped by lake waters. The cuisine is inventive, if sometimes ultra-minimalist (see p127).

Villa Fiordaliso's dining room

2 Ristorante Cracco, Milan

This bastion of fine Milanese cooking was completely overhauled and reopened under the guidance of Carlo Cracco. With two Michelin stars, the menu is adventurous and the wine list exceptional. If the stratospheric prices make you cringe, know that around the corner is Peck, also managed by Cracco, and one of the finest food emporia in Italy, where raw ingredients and prepared dishes can make up a glorious picnic (see p89).

3 Trattoria da Pino, Milan

Genuine Milanese home cooking is the order of the day here. You'll be squeezed in with the locals at this simple place, but it's worth it for the delicious daily specials, combined with bargain prices and great atmosphere (see p89).

4 Trattoria al Porto, Lake Iseo

With its appealing rustic-chic interior and welcoming atmosphere, local specialities make up the menu here. Gabriella cooks up dishes such as lake fish risotto, braised beef with polenta and mushroom gnocchi with a walnut sauce (see p133).

5 Joia, Milan

Swiss chef-owner Pietro Leeman spent time in the Orient before opening Milan's temple of vegetarian cuisine, and many of his dishes have a hint of the exotic that put them in a gourmet category. The wine list is joined by a selection of ciders and organic beers (see p97).

6 Aimo e Nadia, Milan

Aimo and Nadia Moroni are among the top chefs in all Milan. They are fanatical about hunting down the best ingredients, and it shows in such delectables as risotto with pumpkin flowers and truffles. It's well worth the longish haul from the city centre to dine here (see p103).

Vibrant, art-bedecked interior of Aimo e Nadia

Stylish Ristorante Berton

(7) Ristorante Berton, Milan

This minimalist-chic Michelin-starred restaurant fits in perfectly with its futuristic surroundings at Porta Nuova (see p43). The menu includes lots of seafood (see p97).

(8) Il Sole di Ranco, Lake Maggiore

For more than 150 years, the Brovelli family has run an inn and *osteria* in the tiny lakeside village of Ranco, with summertime seating on shaded terraces. The wine list offers more than 1,200 choices, and they'll set up a wine tasting to accompany your *degustazione* (tasting) menu (see p111).

(9) Barchetta, Lake Como

 Restaurants in such touristy towns as Bellagio rarely rise to the level of quality that this has achieved under chef-owner Armando Valli. The signature dish is the *sinfonia degli otto sapori del lago*, a "symphony" of eight lake fishes. For dessert, try the traditional *paradel* – honey ice cream with raisins (see p119).

(10) Don Carlos at the Grand Hotel et de Milan

Named after Verdi's opera, this restaurant offers a highly memorable experience, serving Italian creative cuisine with oriental touches. The walls feature photos and drawings of La Scala and the discreet background music is operatic. Open for dinner only, the kitchen closes at 11:30pm – late for Milan (see p89).

TOP 10 ITALIAN SNACKS

1 Olives
Italy is one of the world's premier olive-growing nations. Enjoy them accompanied by a glass of wine.

2 Panini
Fillings – and a variety of bread – can be chosen when ordering a panino sandwich from a bar or delicatessen.

3 Panzerotti
Baked or fried filled dough crescents from southern Italy but now a Milanese delicacy thanks to Luini (see p89).

4 Gelato
Cool and creamy, Italian gelato comes in all sorts of imaginative and delicious flavourings. Vegan ice-cream is now becoming increasingly popular, too.

5 Granita
Ice granules with a (usually natural) flavouring. Lemon and coffee are popular but there may be a selection.

6 Piadina
This Italian flatbread hails from the Adriatic riviera. Classic fillings include soft cheese with ham and rocket.

7 Tramezzini
These white, crust free sliced-bread sandwiches are surprisingly popular. A "toast" is a toasted sandwich, usually featuring ham and cheese.

8 Bruschetta
A slice of toasted bread topped with garlic and olive oil (*aglio e olio*) or something more substantial.

9 Pasticcini
These mini cakes and biscuits can often be ordered with a coffee or tea for a sweet afternoon snack.

10 Pizzette
Pizzas of every size are everywhere. *Pizzette* are usually small and round, while a *trancio di pizza* is a slice.

Tasty snack-sized *pizzette*

🔟 Cafés and Wine Bars

Cosy, welcoming Bar Magenta

1 Bar Magenta, Milan
MAP K3 ■ Via Carducci 13 at Corso Magenta

This is a lovely corner spot that's a cross between an Irish pub and a Parisian Art Deco café, with a zinc bar, high ceilings, free newspapers and a decent list of dishes along with coffee, cocktails and Guinness on tap.

2 Cova, Milan
The Faccioli family opened Cova near La Scala theatre in 1817 and, though it was later moved to Milan's prime shopping street, Via Montenapoleone, it has remained in the family – and continues to be café of choice for the city's elite. Its home-made pastries, chocolates and sandwiches are some of the most exquisite in town, and they brew up a mean cappuccino to boot. There's an elegant little tearoom with refined service, but since this is still Italy you're also welcome to just run in and toss back an espresso *(see p88)*.

3 Cremeria Bolla, Como
MAP C3 ■ Via Boldoni 6 ■ 031-264-256 ■ www.cremeriabolla.it

Located just behind the Duomo, this long-established café is open all day serving freshly baked croissants for breakfast, pastries and ice cream. Considered the best in town for hazelnut, pistachio and chocolate flavours, Bolla has a faithful following, from both locals and visitors.

4 Bar Jamaica, Milan
MAP L2 ■ Via Brera 32 ■ 02-876-723

This historic Milanese café in the Brera district has long been a haunt of artists, writers and intellectuals. It is also where Mussolini used to read (and correct) articles about himself in the daily newspaper, over a cappuccino. It is busy at all hours, serving drinks from coffee to cocktails, as well as huge salads and hot and cold dishes.

5 Il Marchesino alla Scala, Milan
MAP M3 ■ Piazza della Scala 2 ■ 02-7209-4338 ■ www.marchesi.it

The brainchild of chef Gualtiero Marchesi, credited for master-minding Italian creative cuisine, this bar-restaurant within La Scala includes a sushi bar from where you can watch the action in the kitchen.

6 Zucca (Caffè Miani), Milan
This café opened inside the Galleria Vittorio Emanuele II *(see p70)* in 1868. Verdi and Toscanini would stop by after La Scala shows and King Umberto I declared that it served the best coffee in Milan. Its location at the galleria entrance gives a great view of the Duomo façade *(see p88)*.

Zucca's Art Nouveau interior

(7) Pasticceria Marchesi, Milan

A wonderful old-fashioned café and pastry shop happily "discovered" by many a visitor trekking out to see *The Last Supper*. The decor hasn't changed since 1824, the coffee is quite good and the pastries are favoured by Giorgio Armani *(see p96)*.

(8) Sant'Ambroeus, Milan

Looking every inch the 1936 café, from its wood-panelling to its fabulous pink stucco decorations, Sant'Ambroeus is counted among the great temples of chocolate in Italy. The speciality here is their *ambrogiotti*: an indulgence of dark chocolate wrapped around a filling of zabaglione cream *(see p88)*.

Window display at Sant'Ambroeus

(9) Caffè del Tasso, Bergamo

MAP D3 ■ Piazza Vecchia 3 ■ 035-237-966 ■ www.caffedeltasso.it

For over 500 years, the Tasso has been Bergamo's meeting spot for everyone from princes to rebels. Garibaldi and his red shirts met here, and it was once so notorious that a decree (displayed on the wall) was made in 1845 prohibiting rebellious conversations from taking place.

(10) Bar Portici del Comune, Cremona

MAP E6 ■ Piazza del Comune 2 ■ 335-783-6892

You just can't get a better seat in town than one at an outdoor table set under a lofty medieval arcade with the façade of Cremona's Duomo filling up your panorama.

TOP 10 COCKTAILS AND DRINKS

Fashionable Aperol Spritz

1 Aperol Spritz
This popular bright orange cocktail is everywhere in Italy; it's made with Aperol, Prosecco and soda water.

2 Crodino
A well-known non-alcoholic pre dinner drink, Crodino also has a distinctive orange hue and tangy flavour.

3 Martini Cocktail
This classic cocktail, made with the famous Italian vermouth, gin and lemon juice, is decorated with an olive.

4 Bellini
A refreshing summer cocktail first created in Venice at Harry's Bar, made with Prosecco and peach juice.

5 Amari
A wide range of this traditional brown herb-based digestive is made in Italy.

6 Grappa
This strong, clear after-dinner drink, made using what is left over from the grapes after they have been pressed, has at least 35 per cent alcohol.

7 Campari
Another classic pre dinner drink, distinctive red Campari is often served as a Spritz with Prosecco and soda.

8 Bombardino
Ideal as a mountain winter warmer, Bombardino is served hot. It's made with eggnog and brandy and topped with whipped cream.

9 Americano
Despite its name, this cocktail was first conceived in Italy; made with Campari, red vermouth and soda water.

10 Ugo
Light and refreshing, this tasty cocktail hails from northern Italy and combines Prosecco, elderflower syrup and mint.

Shopping Areas in Milan

Typically stylish display at 10 Corso Como

① 10 Corso Como
MAP L2

This prestige address started out in 1990 as a photography gallery and, over the years a bookshop, a store selling fashion and accessories by innovative designers, a courtyard café-restaurant and a tiny, chic hotel called 3 Rooms have been added (see p95).

② Galleria Vittorio Emanuele II
MAP M3

This glorious 19th-century shopping mall (see p83), though small, houses a little of everything. You'll find class

Glass-domed interior of the Galleria

(Prada) and mass-market (a Ricordi/Feltrinelli superstore of CDs and books). For a shopping break, visit the bastion of la dolce vita that is Zucca in Galleria (see p88).

③ Via Manzoni
MAP M2–3

This boulevard became an epicentre of Milanese fashion when Giorgio Armani opened his gargantuan superstore here in 2000 (see p85). On Manzoni there's everything from the Roman fashions of Davide Cenci (No. 7) to the check-me-out jewellery of Donatella Pellini (No. 20).

④ Corso di Porta Ticinese
MAP K5

Much more unconventional than Milan's other shopping streets, this vibrant road, which ends up near the Navigli district (see pp28–9), has vintage clothing stores as well as small-scale independent shops stocking niche street-wear labels and one-of-a-kind accessories.

⑤ La Rinascente
MAP M4 ▪ Piazza Duomo
▪ www.rinascente.it

Italy's premier department store was founded in 1865 and has always been influential in the development of local society. Elegant yet approachable, departments include homeware and cosmetics as well as clothing from local new designers and unusual accessories. The top floor dining and food hall has unparalleled views of the cathedral next door.

6 Milan's Markets
MAPS J6 (Via Valenza), M1 (Via San Marco), J5 (Papiniano)

The main market is Saturday's Fiera di Sinigaglia on Via Valenza, behind Porta Genova station. Milan's Sunday flea market surrounds the San Donato metro stop in the south. Local markets are on Via San Marco (Mondays and Thursdays), Via Benedetto Marcello (northeast of the Giardini Pubblici) on Tuesdays, and Viale Papiniano near the Navigli (Tuesdays and Saturdays). Markets tend to shut by 1pm, except on Saturdays.

Interior of the food emporium Eataly

7 Quadrilatero d'Oro
MAP L3 ■ Via Sant'Andrea/Via della Spiga/Via Montenapoleone/Via Manzoni

Milan's aptly-named Golden Quad is a quadrangle of streets containing some of the most exclusive branches of top designer stores. Window displays may be sensational or simple but they're always extravagant and oozing glamour, while the respectful hush is regularly broken by the low rumble of Ferraris and Lamborghinis. A must-see even for those who aren't big shoppers.

8 Eataly
MAP L1 ■ Piazza XXV Aprile 10 ■ www.eataly.net

A foodie's paradise housed in a converted theatre, Eataly sells food-related items alongside a vast selection of the highest-quality food from all over Italy, many products sourced from small-scale producers. There are also a dozen specialist eateries and bars, while themed dinners, tastings, courses and other events are organized too.

9 Corso Vittorio Emanuele II
MAP M4–N3

This pedestrian street at the back of the Duomo is lined with arcades and some of the hippest shops in central Milan, including sophisticated brands like Furla, Pollini and Max Mara.

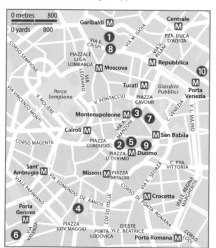

10 Corso Buenos Aires
MAP P1

This long road is where your average Milanese heads to shop. You'll find everything from hand-made men's dress shirts and Richard Ginori china to bootleg records.

🔟 What to Buy

Prada, a Milanese company synonymous with high fashion

1 Designer Clothes

Milan is monumentally important to the world of fashion. Every important label, whether local or based in Paris, Florence or New York, maintains a boutique in Milan. For those whose tastes outstrip their budgets, Milan is also home to some excellent discount outlets.

2 Handbags

Swoon over the designs from Prada and Bottega Veneta, or the less pricey label Coccinelle. Alternatively, plump for one of the many well-made, non-label leather bags, still in great Italian style.

Designer handbags

3 Shoes

Italian footwear ranges from the practical to the gorgeous and outrageous. Seek out the specialist shops, whether it be for an *haute couture* work of art at Ferragamo *(see p86)* or a designer discount bargain from Rufus *(see p95)*.

4 Design Objects

Italian industrial designers are maestros at turning everyday objects such as kettles, lighting systems and juicers into works of art. The often whimsical, usually beautiful and always ergonomically sound results are on sale throughout Italy, or you can go right to the source on Lake Orta. Here, an artisan tradition gave rise in the late 19th century to firms such as Alessi, Bialetti and Lagostina.

5 Linens

Bassetti and Frette offer affordable, stylish linens. The *haute couture* of sheets and tablecloths is represented by Pratesi and, at the pinnacle, Jerusum, which provided the lace-edged linens for Italy's royal family in the 19th century.

6 Art and Antiques

Milan's art dealers offer a rich collection of lesser-known Byzantine and Baroque works and a plethora of 19th-century oils and other relatively affordable art. You'll find 18th-century Venetian chairs, country-style hardwood dressers and Empire-style clocks cluttering the *antichità* shops.

7 Wine

Lombard wines are generally excellent *(see p65)*. Furthermore, the lakes border both the Veneto – home to Valpolicella, Pinot Grigio and Soave – and Piemonte, where the mighty Barolo, Barbaresco and Barbera red wines are crafted.

8 Silk

Como has long been Italy's chief purveyor of finely spun silk fabrics. The Milanese maestros of *haute couture* come to Como to finger the fabrics that will soon be draped across a supermodel's shoulders. These same sought-after silks are available to the public in factory warehouses around Como and in shops across Lombardy.

Como silk of every hue on sale

9 Books

A weighty catalogue of Milanese galleries, a glossy tome of lake scenes or a translation of Manzoni's local literary classic *I Promessi Sposi (see p52)* might be a more treasured souvenir than a sheaf of postcards or trinkets.

10 Jewellery

Though it's not a top European capital of baubles and precious gems, Milan's jewellers hold their own. Seek out the bold creations of Donatella Pellini or the cutting-edge minimalism of Xenia. For something more classic, try Gobbi 1842 and especially Mario Buccellati, a firm that, since 1919, has produced exquisite jewellery, elegant tableware and renowned silver objets d'art.

TOP 10 FASHION HOUSES AND GURUS

Style guru Georgio Armani

1 Armani
Italy's top fashion guru is the master of smart clothes that, for a price tag with far too many zeroes, can help anyone look like a model.

2 Versace
Gianni Versace popularised "violently elegant" designs and costumed many La Scala productions in the 1980s.

3 Prada
The most chillingly expensive of Milan designers, Prada breathed new life into relaxed minimalism with the help of a simple small red stripe.

4 Mila Schön
A giant of fashion who pioneered the double-face fabric in the 1960s.

5 Krizia
Ever an eclectic designer, Mariuccia "Krizia" Mandelli has been flouting trends and winning awards since 1954.

6 Ermenegildo Zegna
Fourth-generation, environmentally aware firm that uses the finest cashmere, merino and mohair in its fabrics.

7 Moschino
An enfant terrible of Milan's fashion scene since way back in 1983.

8 Missoni
This husband-and-wife team has charmed the fashion world since 1953 with their multi-coloured, zigzag knits.

9 Trussardi
Still a family firm, founded by a Bergamasco glove maker in 1910, Trussardi produces classic cuts and gorgeous leather accessories.

10 Ferré
The late Gianfranco Ferré was famous for "architectural" fashion, a look that lingers on in clothing and accessories.

🔟 Milan for Free

1 Every First Sunday
www.beniculturali.it

Many of Italy's state-run museums and archaeological sites don't charge admission fees on the first Sunday of the month. Time your visit right and you could be seeing the Pinacoteca di Brera (see pp16–19) or the Castello Sforzesco museums (see pp20–21) absolutely free. At Lake Garda head to Sirmione for the Grotte di Catullo and Rocca Scaligera (see pp121–2).

Grotte di Catullo at Sirmione

2 Hangar Bicocca
MAP S1 ▪ Via Chiese 2
▪ Open 10am–10pm Thu–Sun
▪ www.hangarbicocca.org

This vast converted factory building is now a centre for contemporary art, with exhibitions by artists from all over the world. Free guided tours, and bicycle tours of the former industrial area of Bicocca, are also available.

Evening visit to Castello Sforzesco

3 Studio Museo Francesco Messina
MAP L4 ▪ Via San Sisto 4
▪ Open 10am–6pm Tue–Sun
▪ www.fondazionemessina.it

This collection of 80 sculptures and other works by Francesco Messina, one of Italy's most talented 20th-century sculptors, is housed in a deconsecrated church.

4 Free Walking Tours
www.milanfreetour.com

Expert local guides lead half-day walking tours taking in most of central Milan's main sites. Available in English or Italian, they should be booked in advance. The same group offers personalized tours for a fee.

5 Street Art

Muri Liberi (free walls) is a city initiative making 100 walls in run-down areas of the city available to street artists. Some of the most intriguing are in an open-air museum called Out, located along Via Pontano.

6 Late Entry at Museums

There's free entry from 2pm every Tuesday afternoon and an hour before closing time on other days (2 hours at Museo del Novecento) at the Museo del Novecento (see p81), Museo del Risorgimento (see p94), Gallerie d'Arte Moderna (see p92) and at the various museums within Castello Sforzesco (see pp20–21).

7 Casa Museo Boschi Di Stefano

MAP S2 ■ Via Giorgio Jan 15
■ Open 10am–6pm Tue–Sun
■ www.fondazioneboschidistefano.it

Around 300 (out of of 2,000) works of outstanding 20th-century Italian art collected by Antonio Boschi and his wife, Marieda Di Stefano, are on show in the couple's former apartment.

8 Galleria Vittorio Emanuele II

This elegant arcade has lavish frescoes and mosaics, including a bull image famous for the tradition of turning three times with a heel on its genitals for luck. Many of the historic shops and bars are museum pieces in themselves *(see p42)*.

Galleria Vittorio Emanuele II mosaic

9 Museo Astronomico-Orto Botanico

MAP M2 ■ Palazzo Brera, Via Brera 28
■ www.ortibotanici.unimi.it;
www.brera.inaf.it

Both the astronomical observatory and the adjacent botanical gardens date from the 18th century and are now owned by the University of Milan. There's a fascinating display of astronomical equipment, whilst the gardens have fun activities for kids.

10 Window-Shopping

It costs absolutely nothing to window-shop the stores of Milan's Golden Quad *(see p71)* where some displays are like a museum of design. The monthly antiques market at Navigli *(see pp28–9)* offers a more vintage browsing experience.

TOP 10 BUDGET TIPS

Luscious market produce on sale

1 Low-cost, good quality food can easily be sourced at neighbourhood delis, bakeries and fruit and vegetable market stalls; Milan's leafy parks are great places for a picnic lunch.

2 Bars often charge for table service, and even more for a terrace table; standing at the bar for a coffee is generally a cheaper option.

3 British National Trust cardholders are entitled to free or discounted at FAI sites including Villa Necchi Campiglio *(see p94)* and Lake Como's Villa Balbianello *(see p114)*.

4 The Tourist Museum Card and MilanoCard are among the city's various multi-day discount cards for museums and/or transport.

5 A carafe of a restaurant's own house wine, served by the quarter, half or full litre, is an inexpensive alternative to a traditional bottle, and often as good.

6 Free access to (often quite lavish) buffets is frequently included in the price of a drink at early evening *aperitivo* time or Happy Hour.

7 Drinks and picnic food can be kept in hotel-room fridges; balconies are ideal for a relaxed meal or snack.

8 Empty plastic bottles can be filled with fresh water at public drinking fountains; *potabile* means drinkable.

9 Over-65s and under-18s (or students with an ID card) can generally benefit from ticket reductions at museums, and discounted family tickets are also often available. Be sure to ask.

10 Fares for fast trains are often much cheaper if booked in advance, either online or at the station.

🔟 Festivals and Events

Carnival crowds in Piazza del Duomo

days when the entire city comes alive with exhibitions and events related to all the latest trends in furniture and interior design.

4 Palio di Legnano
Last Sun in May ▪ www.palio dilegnano.it

Two years after the Lombard League trounced Barbarossa in 1176 (see p38), the town of Legnano began celeb-rating. They're still at it today, putting on a display of pageantry that ends with a horse race.

5 Festa dei Navigli
First Sun in Jun

Milan's trendy Navigli canal district (see pp28–9) celebrates the start of summer on the first Sunday in June by bursting into a street fair with artisan stalls and live music.

1 Carnival
Feb/Mar (ends the first Sat of Lent) ▪ Info: 02-7740-4343

Carnevale in Milan is a combi-nation of religious pomp, fancy-dress parade and Bacchanalian bash. Carnivals elsewhere end on Martedì Grasso ("Fat Tuesday"), but Archbishop St Ambrose decreed that in Milan it should go on until the Saturday. No wonder they made him a saint.

6 Ferragosto
15–31 Aug

The Feast of the Assumption, held on 15 August, is when most Italians head to the beach or lakes for a two-week holiday, and life in the city slows down. Mantua has a celebration of street artists, but Milan virtually shuts down. Only the restaurants and bars of the Navigli tend to stay open.

2 Fashion Week
Jan, Feb, Sep & June

Milan is invaded by models, buyers and media types four times a year who come to the city for fashion week. In mid-January and late June they come for the menswear collections, while February and September are for womenswear.

Model at Fashion Week

3 Milan Furniture Fair
Mid-Apr ▪ Fieramilano Rho, Milan ▪ 02-4997-1 ▪ www.fiera milano.it

Hotels are fully booked when the Salone Internazionale del Mobile, or Milan Furniture Fair, takes the stage in mid-April. Be sure to book early if you want to be present for the six

Chic seating, Milan Furniture Fair

7 **Stresa Festival, Stresa**
Late Aug–early Sep
■ www.stresafestival.eu

Lake Maggiore's gateway to the Borromean Islands (see p109) hosts five musical weeks of concerts in venues throughout the town and along the lake shores.

8 **Grand Prix, Monza**
Grand Prix: 2nd weekend in Sep ■ www.monzanet.it

The biggest Formula One race takes place in mid-September. At other times, you can still watch macho men driving cars at mind-boggling speeds from April through October.

Formula One Grand Prix at Monza

9 **Stringed Instruments Festivals, Cremona**
Late Sep–early Oct ■ Info: Fondazione Antonio Stradivari, Piazza S Omobono 3 ■ 0372-801-801 ■ www.museodelviolino.org

The home of Amati and Stradivari celebrates luthiers and musicians in a series of festivals, concerts, exhibitions and international competitions (see p48).

10 **Opera Season**
Info: 02-7200-3744 ■ tickets: 02-860-775 ■ www.teatroallascala.org

Milan's La Scala (see p82) is the most important opera house in the world, and if you ever doubted that opera was high art, an evening at its 18th-century home will convince you beyond all doubt. The season opens on 7 December – the feast day of Milan's patron saint, Ambrose – and is a momentous occasion in the Milanese social calendar.

TOP 10 FOOD FESTIVALS

Bardolino's food and wine festival

1 Festa dell'Oliva, Torri del Benaco, Lake Garda
This annual festival, held in late January, includes visits to olive mills, tastings and live music in the village.

2 Salon du Chocolat, Milan
Europe's largest congress centre, Mi.Co, hosts this fair in February; initiatives include a chocolate fashion show.

3 Venerdì Gnocolar, Verona
Gnocchi are distributed to all in Piazza San Zeno at this colourful historic fair, held on the Friday before Lent.

4 Sagra del Pesce, Riva di Solto
Tasty Lake Iseo fish dishes are served at this festival, held each July on the western shore of the lake.

5 Tortellini e Dintorni, Valeggio sul Mincio
This event in early September focuses on Valeggio's exquisite tortellini.

6 Sagra Nazionale del Gorgonzola
The blue-veined cheese, from the town of the same name near Milan, is the tasty focus of this September fair.

7 Festival Franciacorta
Each September the top wine-making area near Lake Iseo celebrates with numerous wine-themed events.

8 Festa dell'Uva e del Vino Bardolino, Lake Garda
A lively historic festival in early autumn dedicated to the famous local wine, with food stalls, parades and music.

9 Festa del Riso, Carpiano
Fragrant risotto of all varieties is the focus of this October festival held at Carpiano, just south of Milan.

10 Festa del Torrone, Cremona
Cremona's sweet speciality *torrone*, or nougat, is celebrated each November.

Milan and the Lakes Area by Area

Varenna, a typically charming
waterside village on Lake Como

TOP 10 Milan's Historic Centre

The Centro Storico of Milan is home to the cathedral, opera house, the magnificent royal palace, art-filled private mansions and busy pedestrian boulevards. This historic district was once the Roman city of Mediolanum, though its boundary walls vanished long ago. As well as splendid sights, the historic centre contains a grid of shopping streets around Via Montenapoleone known as the Quadrilatero d'Oro, or "Golden Rectangle", home to numerous top-name designer boutiques.

Pocket watch, Museo Pezzoli

MILAN'S HISTORIC CENTRE

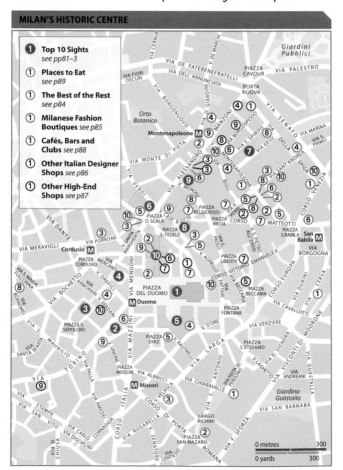

1 Top 10 Sights
see pp81–3

1 Places to Eat
see p89

1 The Best of the Rest
see p84

1 Milanese Fashion Boutiques see p85

1 Cafés, Bars and Clubs see p88

1 Other Italian Designer Shops see p86

1 Other High-End Shops see p87

0 metres 300
0 yards 300

Magnificent interior of Milan's Duomo, with its Great Organ

1 Duomo
MAP M4

The great travel writer H V Morton (see p52) likened Milan's cathedral to a forest within the city, its thickets of columns and high vaulted ceilings providing the citizens with a spot of shade (see pp14–15).

2 Santa Maria presso San Satiro
MAP L4 ▪ Via Speronari 3 ▪ Open 7:30–11:30am, 3:30–6:30pm Mon–Fri, 9am–noon, 3:30–7pm Sat & Sun

Renaissance architect Donato Bramante knew that the only way to squeeze the impression of a Greek cross into a space that only allowed room for a Latin cross was to conduct a layering of stuccoes, angled niches and frescoes behind the altar to give the illusion of a barrel-vaulted presbytery. Another notable feature here is a *Pietà* group by the Lombard sculptor Agostino De' Fondutis (see p41).

3 Pinacoteca Ambrosiana
MAP L4

The art-loving Cardinal Federico Borromeo gave the city one of its greatest treasures when he bequeathed his private collection of works by Leonardo, Titian, Caravaggio and others, including the original cartoon for Raphael's famed *School of Athens* (see p24).

4 Palazzo della Ragione
MAP L4 ▪ Piazza Mercanti ▪ Open for exhibitions ▪ Adm

Milan's 13th-century *broletto* (town hall) is a striking remnant of the Middle Ages (see p42).

5 Palazzo Reale
MAP M4 ▪ Piazza del Duomo 12 ▪ Adm ▪ www.palazzorealemilano.it ▪ Museo del Novecento: Adm; www.museodelnovecento.org

Once home to the Visconti and Sforza families, Milan's Neo-Classical Royal Palace was built under the aegis of Empress Maria Theresa in the 18th century and extended in 1939–56 with the Arengario, a towering pavilion on Piazza Duomo. This now houses the Museo del Novecento, an impressive collection of 20th-century paintings and sculpture. Palazzo Reale is also open for exhibitions.

Façade of the Arengario

Interior of La Scala, viewed from one of its luxurious boxes

6 La Scala
MAP M3 ■ Piazza della Scala
■ www.teatroallascala.org

The world's greatest opera house was built in 1776–8 under the Austrians. It boasts a sumptuous interior, excellent acoustics and a staggering list of premieres *(see p53)*. Half destroyed in World War II, La Scala again became the toast of the town in 1946, when Toscanini presided over its gala reopening.

7 Museo Bagatti Valsecchi
MAP N3 ■ Via S Spirito 10/Via Gesù 5 ■ Open 1–5:45pm Tue–Sun ■ Adm ■ www.museobagatti valsecchi.org

Two Milanese brothers created this Neo-Renaissance palazzo in 1883–94. They acquired as much as they could in the way of tapestries, furnishings and paintings from across Italy, and what they could not obtain in the original they hired Lombard crafts-men to imitate. One room is copied from the ducal palace in Mantua, one from Urbino's ducal seat, another is lifted whole from a palazzo in Sondrio. The overall effect is a mix of Renaissance craftsmanship and Romantic sensibilities.

8 San Fedele
MAP M3 ■ Piazza S Fedele ■ Open 7am–1:15pm, 4:30–6pm Mon–Fri

The single nave construction of this 1559 Jesuit temple would become a blueprint for Lombard churches built in the Counter-Reformation. The interior preserves some fine art, including Il Cerano's *Vision of St Ignatius* and Campi's *Four Saints and Transfiguration*. The sacristy is lined by cabinets by Jesuit Daniele Ferrari, who also carved the pulpit.

San Fedele

MILANESE LUCK

The central floor mosaic in the Galleria Vittorio Emanuele II sports the white-cross-on-red of the House of Savoy (representing Italy's newly crowned king who lent the gallery his name in 1868) and also a bull symbolizing Milan. According to local tradition, the Milanese ensure their good luck by stomping and spinning on the bull's testicles each time they pass.

9 Museo Poldi Pezzoli

MAP M3 ■ Via Manzoni 12
■ Open 10am–6pm Wed–Mon (last
adm 5:30pm) ■ Adm ■ www.
museopoldipezzoli.it

One of the most splendid private
collections in Italy was bequeathed to
the city by Gian Giacomo Poldi Pezzoli
in 1879. Its masterpieces all date from
the last half of the 15th century,
including works by Bellini, Botticelli,
Pollaiolo, Piero della Francesco and
Mantegna. There are 18th-century
Venetian cityscapes by Canaletto and
Guardi, and the *Tapestry of the Hunt*
from Tabriz is celebrated. There is also
a collection of scientific instruments
arms and armour and clocks *(see p45)*.

Pollaiolo at Museo Poldi Pezzoli

10 Galleria Vittorio Emanuele II

MAP M3

Before modern shopping centres and
malls, there were *gallerie*. These late
19th-century high-class shopping
arcades were roofed by the newest
architectural technology of the age:
steel-reinforced glass. Milan's
Industrial Age-cum-Neo-Classical
example connected Piazza del
Duomo with La Scala and was so
successful it spawned an Italy-wide
trend, with copycat *gallerie* popping
up in Naples, Genoa and Rome *(see
p42 & pp85–7 for shops)*.

A DAY IN CENTRAL MILAN

▶ MORNING

Start at 10am by exploring
the stupendous collections of
Pinacoteca Ambrosiana *(see p81)*.

Work your way south to Via Torino
and the jewelbox of a church,
Santa Maria presso San Satiro
(see p81), then walk north up Via
Torino until you reach the Piazza
del Duomo. Continue along the
piazza's western edge and divert
up Via Mercanti to see the raised
porticoes of **Palazzo della
Ragione** *(see p81)*. Now cross the
huge **Duomo** square to enjoy the
marvels of Italy's second-largest
cathedral *(see pp14–15)*. Don't
miss exploring its roof.

Join locals at **Luini** *(see p89)*
for mozzarella-filled doughballs,
then have a drink at **Zucca** *(see
p88)* at the entrance to **Galleria
Vittorio Emanuele II**, the grandest
shopping arcade in Italy.

AFTERNOON

Exit the arcade at Piazza della
Scala, flanked by the opera house
and **Palazzo Marino** *(see p42)*.
Behind the latter is **San Fedele**.
After seeing this, walk northeast
past the **Casa degli Omenoni**
(see p84).

Turn left to visit the excellent
Museo Poldi Pezzoli, then
continue north on Via Manzoni,
admiring its palazzi until you
come to Milan's shopping street,
Via Montenapoleone *(see p71)*.

Shoppers will spend the rest of
the day here; museum hounds
can take in the **Museo Bagatti
Valsecchi**. Both should stop for
drinks at **Cova** *(see p88)*.

See map on p80 ←

The Best of the Rest

 Ca' Granda
MAP M4–5 ■ Via Festa del Perdono 5 ■ Open 7:30am–7:30pm Mon–Fri, 8am–noon Sat

This massive 15th-century building, originally a hospital, is now part of the University of Milan.

2 San Nazaro Maggiore
MAP M5 ■ Piazza S Nazaro in Brolo 5 ■ Open 7:30am–noon, 3:30–6:30pm Mon–Fri, 8am–12:20pm, 3:30–7pm Sat & Sun

St Ambrose's fourth basilica grew in the 16th century, when Bramantino added the Cappella Trivulzio.

3 Torre Velasca
MAP M5 ■ Piazza Velasca 5 ■ No public access

This skyscraper is an oversized 1950s version of medieval tower design (see p43).

4 San Gottardo in Corte
MAP M4 ■ Via Pecorari 2 ■ Open 8am–noon, 2–6pm Mon–Fri, 2–4pm Sat, 8am–noon Sun

This church was founded in 1336 as a chapel for the Palazzo Reale.

5 Museo Teatrale alla Scala
MAP M3 ■ Piazza della Scala ■ Open 9am–noon, 1:30–5pm daily ■ Adm

From scores to costumes, all things related to La Scala (see p82) can be found in this museum (see p44).

 Basilica di San Babila
MAP N3 ■ Piazza San Babila

The Neo-Romanesque façade provides an unusual contrast to the modern shopping area around it.

7 Casa degli Omenoni
MAP M3 ■ Via Omenoni 3 ■ No public access

Sculptor Leoni's 16th-century home has a magnificent façade flanked by a Liberty-style tower (see p43).

8 Casa del Manzoni
MAP M3 ■ Via Morone 1 ■ 02-8646-0403 ■ Open 10am–6pm Tue–Fri, 2–6pm Sat ■ Adm ■ www.casadelmanzoni.it

Manzoni, Italy's greatest 19th-century writer (see p52), lived in this palazzo, now his museum.

9 Gallerie d'Italia
MAP M3 ■ Piazza della Scala 6 ■ 800-167-619 ■ Open Tue–Sun ■ Adm ■ www.gallerieditalia.com

The Brentani and Anguissola Palaces house the private Gallerie d'Italia, which includes masterpieces from the 19th and 20th centuries.

10 Palazzo Morando – Costume Moda Immagine
MAP N3 ■ Via Sant'Andrea 6 ■ Open 9am–1pm, 2–5:30pm Tue–Sun ■ Adm

In an elegant 18th-century town house, Milan's history is documented with art, artifacts and costumes.

Exhibits in the Museo Teatrale alla Scala

Milanese Fashion Boutiques

Versace window display

1 Gianni Versace
MAP N3 ■ Via Montenapoleone 11 (Versus at Via San Pietro all'Orto)
Five floors, with the entire ground level dedicated to accessories. Versace always manages to surprise.

2 Prada
MAP M3 ■ Galleria Vittorio Emanuele II & Via Montenapoleone 8
Central outlets of the firm that transformed a handbag business into the high-fashion success story of the 1990s.

Prada handbag

3 Trussardi
MAP N3 ■ Via Sant'Andrea 5 & Piazza della Scala 5
Founded in 1911, this Bergamo glove-making firm is now one of the top designers of supple leather goods and ready-to-wear fashions.

4 Moschino
MAP N3 ■ Via Sant'Andrea 12 (also Via Durini 14)
Everything from *prêt-à-porter* to jeans from the fashion iconoclast.

5 Dolce & Gabbana
MAP N3 ■ Via Montenapoleone 4
A three-floor luxury retail boutique, with a fantastic interior in green marble, briar-wood and large mirrors.

6 Missoni
MAP N3 ■ Via Montenapoleone 8 (entrance Via Sant'Andrea)
This shop is a riot of colourful, iconic patterned knitwears from Ottavio and Rosita Missoni, who turned the fashion maxims of minimalism and basic black upside down.

7 Tom Ford
MAP M3 ■ Via Verri 3
Synonymous with the resurrection of Gucci in the early 1990s, and later of Yves Saint Laurent, American designer and film director Tom Ford continues to go from strength to strength. This sleek luxury boutique is his first retail outlet in Milan.

8 Krizia
MAP N2 ■ Via della Spiga 23
This Bergamo native delights in contrary fashions: colourful when black is in, miniskirts when conservative hemlines are the rage.

9 Giorgio Armani
MAP M2 ■ Via Manzoni 31
The first mega-department store devoted to just one fashion house – that of Milan's very own guru. The vast space stocks all things Armani, and there's a chic café as well.

10 Ermenegildo Zegna
MAP M2 ■ Via Montenapoleone 27
Detailed perfection in menswear is the watchword in this store, which offers the very best in fabrics and tailoring, plus stylish casual wear.

See map on p80

Other Italian Designer Shops

Frette's showroom, replete with gorgous linens

1 Frette
MAP N3 ▪ Via della Spiga 31

Among the highest-quality linens in all of Italy: everything from towels to pyjamas to sheets and pillowcases.

2 Ferragamo
MAP N3 ▪ Via Montenapoleone 3 (women's) and 20 (men's)

The Florentine cobbler Salvatore Ferragamo raised footwear to a modern art form when he shod Hollywood stars from Greta Garbo to Sophia Loren. Check out the sales in January and July.

3 Alessi
MAP N3 ▪ Via Manzoni 14/16

You'll find kettles, silverware settings and other quirky style items crafted by the top names in international industrial design.

Alessi kitchenware

4 Mario Buccellati
MAP N3 ▪ Via Montenapoleone 23

Since 1919, no two Buccellati jewels have been the same: each gemstone and silver filigree setting is hand-crafted by skilled artisans.

5 Etro
MAP N3 ▪ Via Montenapoleone 5 (fragrances: Via Verri/corner Via Bigli)

Etro's trademark paisley and Pegasus icons abound on silk, cashmere and the finest wools.

6 Valentino
MAP N3 ▪ Via Montenapoleone 20

New York's Metropolitan Museum once mounted a show of Valentino's artistic clothing. Everything is classy, chic and very desirable.

7 Max Mara
MAP N3 ▪ Corso Vittorio Emanuele II

After more than 50 years at the top of their class in womenswear, the Maramotti family's *prêt-à-porter* fashions are more vibrant and wearable than ever.

8 Gucci
MAP N3 ▪ Via Montenapoleone 5 (accessories & café: Galleria Vittorio Emanuele II)

The mating "G"s that once decorated the leather goods of this firm, founded by a Florentine saddlemaker, are a thing of the past, but the quality is still top-notch.

9 Versace Home
MAP M2 ▪ Via Borgospesso 15a

Occupying half the block, this elegant store offers a tempting array of the Versace take on home furnishings.

10 Gio Moretti
MAP N2 ▪ Via della Spiga 4

This boutique offers Giovina Moretti's selection of the best of the season's top fashion and accessories.

Other High-End Shops

 DoDo
MAP M4 ■ La Rinascente,
Piazza Duomo

This Milanese jeweller specializes in gold charms in the shape of animals and flowers. Part of their profits go to support Italian wildlife.

 Cravatterie Nazionali
MAP N3 ■ Via San Pietro
all'Orto 17

A vast selection of ties by Italy's top designers.

3 **Mortarotti**
MAP M3 ■ Via Manzoni 14

Tired of boutique-hopping? Mortarotti is a single shop stocking about a dozen major women's labels: Ferré, Missoni, Roberto Cavalli, Allegri, Eva Branca and more.

A board game for kids at Città del Sole

 Dmag
MAP N3 ■ Via Manzoni 44

In the heart of high fashion sits a cut-price designer outlet, with Fendi scarves, Armani slacks, Prada sweaters and Helmut Lang suits among the bargains waiting to be grabbed. Check daily for bargains on the constantly rotating racks.

5 **Excelsior Milano**
MAP M4 ■ Galleria del Corso 4

This elegant shopping centre hosts big brands such as Tiffany. Fashion, beauty and accessories are to be found upstairs, while downstairs there is a trendy food store selling quality Italian delicacies.

 Ricordi
MAP M3 ■ Galleria Vittorio
Emanuele II

Milan's huge subterranean branch of Italy's premiere chain of music and CD megastores, Ricordi has come a long way since it published the music of Rossini, Verdi, Bellini and Puccini.

 Bocca
MAP M3 ■ Galleria Vittorio
Emanuele II

This longtime resident of the Galleria Vittorio Emanuele II is the place to find beautifully illustrated Italian exhibition catalogues, past and present, as a gift or for your own collection.

8 **Vetrerie di Empoli**
MAP M2 ■ Via
Montenapoleone 22

A glassware boutique selling elegant, high-quality products within a number of themed rooms.

9 **Città del Sole**
MAP L4 ■ Via Torino 57

This is Italy's main chain store for quality educational toys and games. The bright, welcoming store is packed with fun finds.

10 **Gastronomia Peck**
MAP L4 ■ Via Spadari 9

Superlative Milanese grocers since 1883, with three vast floors of meats, cheeses, vegetables, breads, wines and other delicacies. Its pricey restaurant, Cracco, is nearby (see p89).

Cold counter at Gastronomia Peck

See map on p80 ←

Cafés, Bars and Clubs

Taking a break from shopping at the chic D&G Bar Martini

1 D&G Bar Martini
MAP N3 ■ Corso Venezia 15
■ www.dolcegabbana.it ■ €€€

Elegance and style pervade this
bar-bistro in the heart of the fashion
district, as one would expect from
two such glamorous names.

2 Zucca (Caffè Miani)
MAP M3 ■ Galleria Vittorio
Emanuele II & Piazza Duomo 21
■ www.caffemiani.it ■ €

A gorgeous Liberty-style café, with
views of the Duomo, once owned by
the Campari family *(see p68)*.

3 Le Banque
MAP L3 ■ Via Porrone 6 ■
02-8699-6565 ■ www.lebanque.it ■ €

This business people's lunch spot
transforms into a yuppie disco – one
of the few in central Milan – with live
music after 11pm; dress well.

4 Armani Privé
MAP M3 ■ Via Pisoni
■ 02-7231-8655 ■ Closed Mon,
Tue, Sun & Jun–Aug ■ €€

This classy nightclub is inspired by
Japan and has a strict door policy.
Obligatory one drink minimum.

5 Nepentha
MAP M4 ■ Piazza Diaz 1 ■ €

Perennial Milan discotheque just one
block south of the Duomo, where the
chic set come to dine and then dance
the night away.

6 Princi
MAP L4 ■ Via Speronari 6
■ 02-874-797 ■ €

The various branches of Milan's best
bakery all feature traditional wood-
fired ovens and appealing stone and
wood decor. Their range of baked
goods is mouth watering.

7 Sant'Ambroeus
MAP N3 ■ Corso Matteotti 7
■ www.santambroeusmilano.com ■ €

This historic café and tearoom is also
known for making some of the best
chocolates in Italy *(see p69)*.

8 Cova
MAP N3 ■ Via Montenapoleone
8 ■ www.covamilano.com ■ €

Nestling in the heart of Milan's chic
boutique district since 1817, Cova
offers excellent coffee and delicious
pastries *(see p68)*.

9 Savini
MAP M3 ■ Galleria Vittorio
Emanuele II ■ 02-7200-3433 ■ €€€

This long-established eatery has a
café and *pasticceria* as well as an
excellent restaurant.

10 Signorvino
MAP M3 ■ Piazza Duomo ■ €€

The Milan branch of this collection of
wine bars stands in a prime position
on Piazza Duomo, just to the left of
the city's iconic cathedral. Come for
advice on wines to buy or enjoy here.

Places to Eat

PRICE CATEGORIES
For a three-course meal for one with half
a bottle of wine (or equivalent meal),
taxes and extra charges.

€ under €35   €€ €35–€60   €€€ over €60

1 **Trattoria da Pino**
MAP N4 ■ Via Cerva 14
■ 02-7600-0532 ■ Lunch only
■ Closed Sun ■ No credit cards ■ €
An *osteria* serving simple, traditional
dishes in a room behind the street-
front bar, using fresh seasonal ingredients (*see p66*).

2 **Don Carlos at the Grand Hotel et de Milan**
MAP M2 ■ Via Manzoni 29 ■ 02-7231-
4640 ■ Closed lunch & Aug ■ €€€
Open for dinner only, and perfect for
a post-opera meal (*see p67*).

3 **Al Cantinone**
MAP M3 ■ Via Agnello 19
■ 02-863-015 ■ Closed 1 wk Aug
■ €€€
This Lombard–Tuscan hybrid is set
in two classically elegant rooms.

4 **Ristorante Cracco**
MAP L4 ■ Via Victor Hugo 4
■ 02-876-774 ■ Closed Sun, Aug &
Christmas ■ €€€
Minimalist chic modern dining,
complete with liveried doorman
and astronomic prices (*see p66*).

Chefs at work at Ristorante Cracco

5 **Luini**
MAP M3 ■ Via S Radegonda 16
■ 02-8646-1917 ■ Closed Sun & Mon
from 3pm ■ No credit cards ■ €
Luini may serve only *panzerotti*
(pockets of stuffed dough), but
locals flock here to eat them.

6 **Don Lisander**
MAP M2 ■ Via Manzoni 12a
■ 02-7602-0130 ■ €€€
Creative regional, Tuscan and French
cuisines in palatial surroundings.

Charmingly elegant Don Lisander

7 **Rinascente Food Court**
MAP M3 ■ Piazza del Duomo
■ 02-885-2471 ■ €€
Enjoy great views as well as no fewer
than seven options to choose from.

8 **Hostaria Borromei**
MAP L4 ■ Via Borromei 4
■ 02-8645-3760 ■ Closed Sun lunch
■ €€€
Milanese and Italian dishes using
seasonal ingredients are key here.

9 **La Vecchia Latteria**
MAP L4 ■ Via dell'Unione 6
■ 02-874-401 ■ Closed Sun ■ €
This welcoming, lunch-only spot
serves a range of tasty vegetarian
dishes and luscious desserts.

10 **Trussardi alla Scala**
MAP M3 ■ Piazza della Scala 5
■ 02-8068-8264 ■ Closed Sat lunch &
Sun ■ €€€
Creative cuisine and a terrific wine
list make for a fine dining experience.

See map on p80 ⬅

🔟 Northern Milan

Etruscan cinerary urn in the Civico Museo Archeologico

Leonardo da Vinci's world-famous fresco, the city's best parks and great museums are the highlights of this area. Three museums trace art from the medieval period (at the Castello Sforzesco) through the golden era of the Renaissance (at the Brera) to Modernism (at the Villa Belgiojoso Bonaparte). Aside from the cultural hightlights, this part of town is also a great place for bargain shoppers, from warehouses lining the street south of the central railway station to the huge shopping boulevard of Corso Buenos Aires.

NORTHERN MILAN

Certosa di Garegnano frescoes

1 Certosa di Garegnano

MAP R2 ■ Via Garegnano 28
■ Open 8am–noon, 3:30–5:30pm daily

The 14th-century Carthusian abbey has largely vanished under Milan's suburbs, but its church of Santa Maria Assunta survives. It has a fine late Renaissance façade, and the interior was beautifully frescoed by Daniele Crespi in 1629 with stories of the Carthusian order.

2 San Simpliciano

MAP L2 ■ Piazza S Simpliciano 7 ■ Open 9am–noon, 2:15–7pm Mon–Fri; 9:30am–7pm Sat & Sun

One of four great basilicas built by St Ambrose in the 4th century (and finished by its namesake in 401) is popularly dedicated to the Anaunia Martyrs. The external walls are mostly original; the interior was renovated in the 11th and 12th centuries, and frescoed with a rainbow of angels and a *Coronation of the Virgin* by Bergognone in 1515. There are also patches of a late 14th-century fresco still visible in a chapel off the choir.

3 Castello Sforzesco

MAP K2

Milan's vast fortress-castle complex squats at the northwest corner of the historic centre. It is an intriguing combination of oversized courtyards, lithe towers and medieval nooks and crannies (see pp20–21).

Castello Sforzesco

	Top 10 Sights see pp91–3
1	Places to Eat see p97
1	The Best of the Rest see p94
1	Shops see p95
1	Cafés, Bars and Clubs see p96

THE ANAUNIA MARTYRS

Three Byzantine missionaries, Sisino, Alessandro and Martirio, were sent by St Ambrose to Bishop Vigilio of Trent. Vigilio assigned them to convert pagans of the Trentino Alpine valleys. But locals of the Anaunia region were having none of it, and stoned the missionaries to death in 397, making them the region's first church martyrs.

4 Parco Sempione

MAP K2 ▪ Piazza Sempione ▪ Park: open 6:30am–1 hour past sunset daily; Aquarium: open 9am–5:30pm Tue–Sun ▪ www.acquario civicomilano.eu

Milan's largest park started life as 15th-century ducal gardens, though its layout dates from the late 19th century. An aquarium is housed in a 1906 Liberty-style structure, and the triumphal Arco della Pace is also located in the park (see p94).

5 Pinacoteca di Brera

MAP M2

In Northern Italy, this gallery is second only to Venice's Accademia (though the Brera has more variety). Since Napoleon inaugurated the collection, it has been housed in the Jesuits' Palazzo di Brera. It includes works by Piero della Francesca, Raphael, Bellini, Mantegna and Caravaggio (see pp16–19).

Dome of Santa Maria delle Grazie

6 Santa Maria delle Grazie

MAP J3 ▪ Piazza S Maria delle Grazie ▪ Church: open 7am–noon, 3–7pm Mon–Sat, 7:30am–12:15pm, 3:30–8:15pm Sun

Leonardo's extraordinary fresco, *The Last Supper*, adorns a wall of the convent refectory (see pp12–13) and is the chief attraction. Other features include a magnificent Renaissance tribune, possibly designed by Bramante, who did the cloister and probably the main portal, as well.

7 Villa Belgiojoso Bonaparte–Galleria d'Arte Moderna

MAP N2 ▪ Via Palestro 16 ▪ Open 9am–1pm, 2–5:30pm Tue–Sun ▪ Adm ▪ www. gam-milano.com

Milan's Neo-Classical (1790) "Royal Villa" housed Napoleon in 1802 and Marshal Radetzky until 1858. It is now an art gallery, with works by Romantic master Hayez; Neo-Classical sculptor Canova, whose bust of Napoleon sits in the stairwell; Morandi, Corot, Gauguin, van Gogh and Picasso (see p44). The villa is set in lovely English-style gardens.

Crivelli triptych in the Pinacoteca di Brera

⑧ Civico Museo Archeologico

MAP K3 ■ Corso Magenta 15 ■ Open 9am–5:30pm Tue–Sun ■ Adm

A few pieces in an otherwise modest collection make this worth a stop. The best are the 4th-century glass Trivulzio Cup and a stunning silver platter from the same period with reliefs of the deities of earth, sky, water and the zodiac. An exhibition is devoted to urban planning and architecture in Milan from the 1st to the 4th century AD. In the 15th-century cloisters, damaged by bombs during World War II, are a pair of brick towers from the Imperial-era city.

Cimitero Monumentale tombs

⑨ Cimitero Monumentale

MAP R2 ■ Piazza Cimitero Monumentale ■ Open 8am–6pm Tue–Sun

Milan's vast 19th-century cemetery is filled with Art Nouveau tombs of Milan's top families – a free map shows where such notables as Arturo Toscanini rest. There's a pantheonic monument and a memorial to the Jews deported by the Nazis.

⑩ San Maurizio al Monastero Maggiore

MAP K3 ■ Corso Magenta 15 ■ Open 9:30am–5:30pm Tue–Sun

The sober grey 16th-century façade conceals a magnificent interior with remarkable cycles of Renaissance frescoes. The most striking, by Bernardino Luini, adorn the partition which divides the public area from the section where cloistered nuns once lived. The church's organ, which dates back to 1554, is regularly used for concerts.

TOURING THE GREAT MUSEUMS OF NORTHERN MILAN

[map showing: San Simpliciano, Latteria San Marco, San Marco, Museo di Storia Naturale, Castello Sforzesco, Pinacoteca di Brera, Villa Belgiojoso Bonaparte, Villa Necchi Campiglio, Panino Giusto]

▶ MORNING

There are two major museums in this itinerary, so it's advisable to start your day off early at the **Castello Sforzesco** *(see p91)* when it opens at 9am. Work your way up to **San Simpliciano** *(see p91)* by around 11am, then make your way southeast to the church of **San Marco** *(see p94)*.

Continue up Via San Marco to have lunch at **Latteria San Marco** *(see p97)*, one of Milan's great simple *trattorie*, then head back down the same street, cross Via Pontaccio, and prepare to plunge into the vast art collections of the **Pinacoteca di Brera**.

AFTERNOON

If you're an art fan, you'll probably spend the rest of the afternoon at the Pinacoteca, ready for a *passeggiata* (stroll) and dinner when you emerge near closing time. But if it doesn't grab you, knock off after 90 minutes and you'll have time to continue east along Via Fatebenefratelli to Piazza Cavour.

From Piazza Cavour, go down Via Palestro to **Villa Belgiojoso Bonaparte**, then call in at the **Museo di Storia Naturale** *(see p94)* to view dinosaur skeletons and wonderfully outdated 19th-century dioramas. Stroll over to Via Mozart to see how the sophisticated Milanese industrialist class lived at **Villa Necchi Campiglio** *(see p94)*, with its important art collections.

Finally, to round off a full and busy day, head for your dinner reservations at **Panino Giusto** *(Via Marcello Malpighi 3)*.

See map on pp90–91 ←

The Best of the Rest

1 Museo del Risorgimento
MAP M2 ▪ Via Borgonuovo 23
▪ Open 9am–1pm, 2–5:30pm Tue–Sun ▪ Adm

Find out about the heroes of Italy's 19th-century *risorgimento* (unification) movement at this museum.

2 San Siro (Stadio Meazza)
MAP R2 ▪ Via Piccolomini 5
▪ Open for matches ▪ Adm ▪ Museum: Gate 14, Mon–Sat, adm

"The Scala of football", which is shared by rivals Inter and AC Milan.

3 Villa Necchi Campiglio
MAP P3 ▪ Via Mozart 14
▪ Open 10am–6pm Wed–Sun ▪ Adm

This is an elegant 1930s villa with important paintings by masters such as Canaletto and Tiepolo *(see p43)*.

4 Museo di Storia Naturale
MAP P2 ▪ Corso Venezia 55
▪ Open 9am–5:30pm Tue–Sun

Dinosaurs and taxidermied creatures are among the exhibits at the natural history museum.

5 Palazzo Litta
MAP K3 ▪ Corso Magenta 24
▪ Open for exhibitions

Italy's state railway headquarters and a theatre occupy the expansive Rococo palazzo near *The Last Supper*.

6 Trienniale Design Museum
MAP J2 ▪ Viale Alemagna 6
▪ Open 10:30am–8:30pm Tue–Sun ▪ Adm ▪ www.triennale.org

Design in all its forms, including inventive everyday items, is on display at this museum on the edge of Parco Sempione. Annual thematic displays begin each spring *(see p42)*.

7 Arco della Pace
MAP J1 ▪ Piazza Sempione

Luigi Cagnola built this magnificent triumphal arch in 1807 for Napoleon to pass through when visiting Milan. It didn't get finished quite in time and was inaugurated instead by a bemused Habsburg emperor.

8 Piazza Gae Aulenti
MAP R2

Named after the architect of the Musée d'Orsay in Paris, this modern piazza by the Garibaldi railway station offers a range of shops and entertainment venues. It is a great place to grab a bite to eat or wander around the shops.

9 Ippodromo
MAP R2 ▪ Via Piccolomini 2
▪ Open 9:30am–6pm daily

In 1999, Milan's horse track became home to a bronze horse cast by an American foundation determined to bring to fruition Leonardo da Vinci's oft-sketched equine tribute to Lodovico "Il Moro" Sforza *(see p39)*.

10 San Marco
MAP N2 ▪ Piazza S Marco 2
▪ Open 7am–noon, 4–7pm daily

Very little is left of the 1254 church, dedicated to St Mark in thanks for Venice's aid in defeating Barbarossa *(see p38)*, but some 13th- and 15th-century frescoes remain on show.

Fragments of fresco in San Marco

Shops

Stylish display of items for the home at Post-Design

1 Post-Design
MAP L1 ▪ Via della Moscova 27

This chic store is a purveyor of the whimsical, stunning design objects produced by Milan's Memphis group, founded in 1981 by Ettore Sottsass and other young designers.

2 10 Corso Como
MAP L2 ▪ Corso Como 10
▪ www.10corsocomo.com

While her sister served as editor of Italian *Vogue*, Carla Sozzani opened this boutique of expensive, eminently fashionable luxury labels on everything from clothes and accessories to books and kitchenware *(see p70)*.

3 Surplus
MAP L1 ▪ Corso Garibaldi 7

If you feel some fashions just never go out of style, visit Milan's top shop for second-hand and reproduction vintage couture since 1979.

4 Cotti
MAP L1 ▪ Via Solferino 42
▪ www.enotecacotti.it

Nearly 1,500 Italian wines, *grappas* (grape-based brandies) and other spirits are stuffed into this gourmet foods shop, established in 1952.

5 Emporio Isola
MAP R2 ▪ Via Prina 11

This is a discount outlet for noted clothing firms. Products are high quality and a wide range of styles, varying from elegant to pure chic, are available. Many bargains are on offer.

6 Dolce e Gabbana
MAP P2 ▪ Corso Venezia 15

Housed in an old historical mansion, this ultra-chic men's apparel store includes a bar, restaurant, barber's shop and grooming centre.

7 Boggi
MAP P1 ▪ Corso Buenos Aires 1

Boggi has been dressing the Milanese for years, providing its discerning with classy clothing and footwear at reasonable prices.

8 Furla
MAP P1 ▪ Corso Buenos Aires/
corner Via Omboni

Located towards the Porta Venezia end of this very long shopping street, Furla provides a constant flow of fashion-forward ideas in handbags.

9 Emporio Moda
MAP S2 ▪ Via Vitruvio 9

Bargain-basement prices on brand-name clothing. Major-label dresses under €150, suits under €200.

10 Rufus
MAP S2 ▪ Via Vitruvio 35

You'll find great discounts on designer shoes here, with some top names coming in at under €90 a pair.

See map on pp90–91

Cafés, Bars and Clubs

1 Pasticceria Marchesi
MAP K3 ■ Via Santa Maria alla Porta 11a ■ 02-862-770 ■ €

This is a delightfully old-world café and chocolatier not far from *The Last Supper (see p69)*.

2 Triennale DesignCafé
MAP J2 ■ Milan Triennale, Viale Alemagna ■ 02-8754-41 ■ Closed Mon ■ €€

Masterminded by Carlo Cracco, whose eponymous restaurant *(see p66)* has two Michelin stars, this café-restaurant with splendid views of Parco Sempione is a great place for a light lunch *(see p94)*.

3 Just Cavalli Caffè
MAP J2 ■ Between Via Shakespeare and Via Cameons, Parco Sempione ■ €–€€

If Roberto Cavalli's in-your-face approach to fashion appeals to you, you will love this lively café, with its leopard-skin-patterned sofas. There is another Cavalli café in the store in Via della Spiga.

4 Bar Radetzky
MAP L1 ■ Largo La Foppa 5 ■ €

This minimalist café has been around for many years, good for a quick espresso in the morning and an *aperitivo* in the evening.

5 Bar Bianco
MAP K2 ■ Viale Ibsen, Parco Sempione ■ 02-8699-2026 ■ €

A summer-only venue, this bar in the park is open till midnight, with the clientele switching from mothers and children to the city's trendiest out for dinner and cocktails.

6 Alcatraz
MAP L1 ■ Via Valtellina 25 ■ 02-6901-6352 ■ Closed Jun–Sep ■ €–€€ (ticket price varies)

Milan's biggest club, staging top bands visiting Milan *(see p62)*.

7 Hollywood
MAP L2 ■ Corso Como 15 ■ 338-505-5761 ■ Closed Mon ■ €

Fashion models and designers claim Hollywood as theirs *(see p63)*.

8 Cantina Isola
MAP R2 ■ Via Paolo Sarpi 30 ■ 02-331-5249 ■ Closed Mon ■ €

A huge range of bottles lines the shelves at this historic wine store and bar and it's possible to ask for just a glass of all but the most prestigious.

9 Blue Note
MAP R2 ■ Via Borsieri 37 ■ 02-6901-6888 ■ Closed Mon (Oct–Mar), Jun–Aug ■ €€€

This famous club gives music lovers the chance to listen to some of the greatest jazz talents live *(see p63)*.

10 Ricci
MAP N1 ■ Piazza Repubblica 27 ■ €€

With TV chef Joe Bastianich and model Belen Rodriguez at the helm, historic Ricci oozes glamour.

Sleek bar area at stylish Ricci

Places to Eat

PRICE CATEGORIES
For a three-course meal for one with half a bottle of wine (or equivalent meal), taxes and extra charges.
....
€ under €35   €€ €35–€60   €€€ over €60

Da Abele's welcoming dining room

1 Da Abele
MAP R2 ▪ Via Temperanza 5 ▪ 02-261-3855 ▪ Closed lunch & Mon ▪ €€€
Perfect for dinner if you love risotto, with three choices that change daily. Slightly off the beaten track and popular with locals.

2 Joia
MAP P1 ▪ Via P Castaldi 18 ▪ 02-204-9244 ▪ Closed Sun, Aug, Christmas ▪ €€€
Milan's premier vegetarian restaurant serves brilliant meals even a sworn carnivore will love (see p66).

Tasting plate, Joia

3 Pizzeria Grand'Italia
MAP L1 ▪ Via Palermo 5 ▪ 02-877-759 ▪ €
Enjoy a slice of some of the best pizza in town at this popular pizzeria.

4 Ristorante Berton
MAP N1 ▪ Via Mike Bongiorno 13 ▪ 02-6707-5801 ▪ Closed Sun ▪ €€€
Run by one of Italy's top chefs, Berton serves amazing food in a refined modern setting. For an even more memorable experience book the special table in the kitchen.

5 Latteria San Marco
MAP M1 ▪ Via San Marco 24 ▪ 02-659- 7653 ▪ Mon–Fri only ▪ Closed Aug ▪ No credit cards ▪ €€
This Brera district trattoria has become so famous you must join the queue early to enjoy the simple Milanese fare.

6 Dhaba
MAP N1 ▪ Via P Castaldi 22 ▪ 02-201-315 ▪ €€
Try one of Milan's oldest Indian restaurants for excellent-value tandoori and curries.

7 Tipica Osteria Pugliese
MAP P1 ▪ Via Tadino 5 ▪ 02-2952-2574 ▪ Closed Mon ▪ €€€
Friendly place with simple, hearty fare from Apulia in southern Italy.

8 Ratanà
MAP S2 ▪ Via Gaetano de Castillia 28 ▪ 02-8712-8855 ▪ €€
A former railway building serves a great choice of local dishes, including *Mondeghili* meatballs.

9 Trattoria Alla Cucina delle Langhe
MAP L1 ▪ Corso Como 6 ▪ 02-6554-279 ▪ Closed 3 wks Aug ▪ €€€
This long-established restaurant serves Piedmontese and Lombard classics on its main floor and more informal fare upstairs.

10 Antica Trattoria della Pesa
MAP L1 ▪ Viale Pasubio 10 ▪ 02-655-5741 ▪ Closed Sun ▪ €€
A historic restaurant, dating from 1880, serving traditional Milanese fare in a charming period setting.

See map on pp90–91

🔟 Southern Milan

The city south of the historic core is dominated by the majority of Milan's most impressive churches: ancient Sant'Ambrogio and majestic San Lorenzo Maggiore; Sant'Eustorgio, with its remarkable carvings and paintings; the Renaissance piles of Santa Maria della Passione and Santa Maria presso San Celso; and the quirky 18th-century cloverleaf of La Besana. There's also the fantastic Science and Technology Museum, housed in a former convent; within its broad scope, the museum pays homage to Leonardo da Vinci's oft-overlooked scientific genius with an excellent display of his technical drawings and models. Further to the south stretch the Navigli canals, once a centre of Milanese commerce and now host to the city's liveliest nightlife and dining scene.

Statue of Constantine at San Lorenzo Maggiore

SOUTHERN MILAN

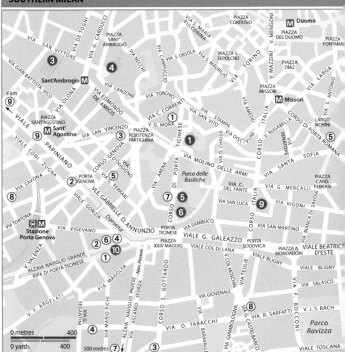

Mosaics in San Lorenzo Maggiore

1 San Lorenzo Maggiore

MAP L5 ■ Corso di Porta Ticinese 39 ■ Open 7:30am–6:30pm Mon, Fri & Sat, 12:30–2:30pm Tue–Thu, 9am–7pm Sun ■ Chapel: open 9am– 6:30pm daily; adm ■ www.san lorenzomaggiore.com

A free-standing row of 16 Corinthian columns – once part of a 2nd-century temple – sets San Lorenzo's frontal piazza off from the road. The vast interior of the church was built on a circular plan, with a ring-shaped ambulatory and raised women's gallery, which often marked such early churches. The chapel has 4th-century mosaics, a 3rd-century sarcophagus and a Roman portal.

2 Santa Maria della Passione

MAP P3 ■ Via Bellini 2 ■ Open 7:30am–noon, 3:30–6:15pm Mon–Fri, 9am–12:30pm, 3:30–6:30pm Sat & Sun

This modest Greek-cross church of 1486–1530 was elongated with a massive nave and deep chapel niches in 1573 to make it the second largest church in Milan. Its interior is dominated by the work of Daniele Crespi: a portrait of San Carlo in the first chapel on the left, most of the Passion series below the cupola at the crossing and the organ doors.

3 Museo Nazionale della Scienza e della Tecnologia – Leonardo da Vinci

MAP J4 ■ Via San Vittore 21 ■ Open 9:30am–4:30pm Tue–Fri, 9:30am–6pm Sat & Sun ■ Adm ■ www.museoscienza.org

The National Science and Technology museum's subtitle refers to the wooden scale models of Leonardo's inventions, which fill the main hall. Also worth seeing are the telecommunications work of Marconi, plus displays on physics, cinematography and electricity and the Enrico Toti submarine (see p44).

Museo Nazionale della Scienza

1 **Top 10 Sights**
see pp99–101

1 **Places to Eat**
see p103

1 **Shops and Nightspots**
see p102

Sant'Ambrogio's handsome cloistered atrium

④ Sant'Ambrogio
MAP K4

Second only to the Duomo among Milan's great churches (and, to many, more beautiful), this 4th-century basilica, has a cloistered entryway, Paleochristian mosaics, medieval carvings and Renaissance frescoes (see pp26–7).

⑤ Museo Diocesano
MAP K5 ■ Corso di Porta Ticinese 95 ■ Open 10am–6pm Tue–Sun ■ Adm ■ www.museodiocesano.it

This museum houses important works from churches across Milan and Lombardy. In addition to numerous small panels by the 14th- and early 15th-century post-Giotto Gothic schools of central Italy, it holds 17th-century Flemish tapestries and some fine altarpieces. Among these are Hayez's *Crucifixion with Mary Magdalene* and Tintoretto's *Christ and the Adulterer*.

Altarpiece, Museo Diocesano

⑥ Sant'Eustorgio
MAP K6 ■ Piazza S Eustorgio ■ Open 7:30am–noon, 3:30–6:30pm daily ■ Museum: open 10am–6pm

The chapels opening off the right side of this ancient church were added between the 11th and 13th centuries, and frescoed in the 1300s and 1400s – Bergognone provided the triptych in the first one. The immense Arc of St Peter Martyr in the magnificent Portinari Chapel (see p41) was carved by Balduccio.

⑦ Abbazia di Chiaravalle
MAP S3 ■ Via S Arialdo 102 ■ Open 9am–noon, 2:30–5pm Tue–Sat, 2:30–5pm Sun

A countryside abbey now surrounded by suburban Milan, Chiaravalle has survived the centuries since its construction (between 1172 and 1221) remarkably well. Its lovely Romanesque architecture is enhanced by 15th- and 16th-century murals and a Luini *Madonna with Child* in the right transept.

⑧ Rotonda di Via Besana
MAP P5 ■ Via Besana 12 ■ Open 10am–7pm Sat, Sun & hols; 5–6:30pm Tue–Fri ■ Adm ■ www.muba.it

Situated just south of Porta Vittoria, this Greek-cross church, dating from 1713, houses the MUBA children's museum (see p60). It is surrounded by a small green park bounded by a lovely rosette-shaped cloister.

⑨ Santa Maria presso San Celso

MAP L6 ▪ Corso Italia 37
▪ Open 7am–noon & 4–6:30pm daily

The word *"presso"* reflecting its proximity to the Romanesque San Celso, this Renaissance church shot up with remarkable speed between 1493 and 1506. Its most alluring aspect is the cloister-like court before the entrance, designed by Cesare Cesarino and considered one of the best examples of early 16th-century architecture in Milan.

Canal cruiser in the Navigli district

⑩ Navigli

MAP K6

Milan needed a port so in the 12th century the Naviglio Grande – a 50-km/30-mile canal linking the city to Lake Maggiore – was created; the Naviglio Pavese (that connects Milan to Pavia) was added at the end of the 14th century. Today, the Navigli district is Milan's liveliest neighbourhood. Its old warehouses contain chic apartments and its towpaths are lined with restaurants, bars and shops. It even stays open during the dog days of August *(see p76)*.

CANAL CRUISES

The tourist office sponsors twice-daily Navigli cruises (book ahead) with an audio CD to tell the story of these canals. On Saturdays this becomes a Cultural Excursion and on Sundays a Nature Tour, both ranging further afield with the aid of buses. Tours last about 4 hours. See www.navigililombardi.it.

A DAY WITH LEONARDO

▶ MORNING

The influence of the Renaissance genius pervades the city of Milan. Begin your day at the Cordusio metro stop, then walk west on Via Meravigli to the corner with Via S Maria alla Porta for a cappuccino at **Pasticceria Marchesi** *(see p96)*. Continue west, and pop into the **Civico Museo Archeologico** *(see p93)* for a few minutes of tranquil historical browsing.

Head to **Santa Maria delle Grazie** *(see p92)*. You'll have made reservations long in advance for early admission to *The Last Supper (see pp12–13)*, so take plenty of time to fully appreciate Leonardo's art.

Go east along Corso Magenta to Via Carducci to relax at the Art Nouveau **Bar Magenta** *(see p68)*.

AFTERNOON

Turn down Via Carducci four long blocks to Via San Vittore (you'll see across the street the Pusterla di S Ambrogio, a remnant of the medieval city gates) and turn right for the **Museo della Scienza e della Tecnologia** *(see p99)*.

At around 3:30pm, double back along Via S Vittore to S Ambrogio. Trek down Via Edmondo De Amicis to Corso della Porta Ticinese, and visit the magnificent **San Lorenzo Maggiore** *(see p99)*. Peruse the works in the **Museo Diocesano**, then continue along to **Sant'Eustorgio**.

The atmospheric **Navigli** district nearby is the perfect setting for a relaxing evening, ending up with a meal at **El Brellin** *(see p103)*.

See map on pp98–9

Shops and Nightspots

Vintage finds at Cavalli & Nastri

1 Cavalli & Nastri
MAP K5 ■ Gian Giacomo Mora 12

Vintage designer clothing for men and women, hand-picked for quality and condition. The favourite haunt of stylists and the stylish. There is another branch at Via Brera 2.

2 Coin
MAP J5 ■ Piazza Cantore 12

This large department store near Porta Genova railway station sells all the most popular fashion and home-accessory brands.

3 Biffi
MAP J5 ■ Corso Genova 6

All the major labels for men and women, including whatever's hot this season, selected by Mrs Biffi.

4 Apollo Club
MAP K6 ■ Via Giosuè Borsi 9 ■ 02-8942-0969 ■ Closed Sun ■ €€

This recent edition to the Navigli nightlife scene offers cocktails, dining and dancing in a classy retro interior. There are often live bands on Saturdays, while Fridays feature indie-electro sounds.

5 Danese
MAP M5 ■ Piazza San Nazaro in Brolo 5 ■ Closed Mon lunch, Sun & Aug

Selling furniture icons of Italian industrial design from greats such as Bruno Munari and Enzo Mari, this cool, stylish store is a must-visit for design enthusiasts.

6 Navigli Antiques Market
MAP K6 ■ Naviglio Grande

This vast market is held on the last Sunday of the month, stretching along each side of the Naviglio Grande canal as well as down some adjacent side streets *(see p29)*.

7 Special Milano
MAP K6 ■ Corso di Porta Ticinese 80 ■ Closed Sun & Mon

In one of the hippest areas in town, this streetwear shop stocks clothes from major international brands. Its sister store Dictionary, aimed at a more fashion-conscious clientele, is at No. 46 on the same street.

Live music at Lime Light

8 Lime Light
MAP R2 ■ Via Castelbarco 11 ■ 342-0919-739 ■ €

A disco owned by a group of Premier League footballers. The DJs spin everything from revival pop to salsa.

9 Viale Papiniano Market
MAP J5 ■ Viale Papiniano ■ 9am–5pm Tue & Sat

For designer bargains, head for Viale Papiniano, with its many keenly priced stalls offering top brands.

10 Il Salvagente
MAP S2 ■ Via Fratelli Bronzetti 16

The best discount outlet in Milan, with two floors of clothing, shoes and bags at about 50 per cent discount.

→ *See map on pp98–9*

Places to Eat

PRICE CATEGORIES

For a three-course meal for one with half a bottle of wine (or equivalent meal), taxes and extra charges.

€ under €35   €€ €35–€60   €€€ over €60

Ponte Rosso

MAP J6 ■ Ripa di Porta Ticinese 23 ■ 02-837-3132 ■ Closed Sun eve, 2 wks Aug ■ €€€

This cheery Navigli canalside trattoria serves dishes from Milan and Trieste.

2 El Brellin

MAP J6 ■ Alzaia Naviglio Grande 14 ■ 02-5810-1351 ■ €€€

Hearty *cassoeûla* and *ossobuco* with saffron-flavoured Milanese risotto are among the traditional specialities served at this quaint Navigli tavern.

3 Contraste

MAP K6 ■ Via Giuseppe Meda 2 ■ 02-4953-6597 ■ €€€

The young chefs aim to surprise and delight diners with dishes that look amazing and taste even better.

4 Premiata Pizzeria

MAP K6 ■ Via Alzaia Naviglio Grande 2 ■ 02-8940-0648 ■ €

This is Navigli's most popular pizzeria, with semi-industrial decor and a terrace.

5 Orto – Erbe e Cucina

MAP K6 ■ Via Gaudenzio Ferrari 3 ■ 02-8366-0716 ■ Closed Mon–Fri lunch, 1 wk Aug, Christmas ■ €

Elegant dishes, many vegetarian, incorporate home-grown herbs.

6 Da Giacomo

MAP P3 ■ Via Sottocorno 6 ■ 02-76023313-189 ■ Closed 2 wks Aug, Christmas ■ €€€

Superb fresh fish, grilled meats and and traditional Milanese *cotoletta*, in an Art Deco setting. Book ahead.

7 Sadler

MAP R3 ■ Via Ascanio Sforza 77 ■ 02-5810-4451 ■ Closed Sun, 1 wk Jan, 2 wks Aug ■ €€€

Claudio Sadler, one of the top chefs in Milan, melds modern techniques sublimely with regional cuisine.

8 Trattoria Aurora

MAP J5 ■ Via Savona 23 ■ 02- 8940-4978 ■ Closed Mon ■ €€

Traditional restaurant with a long-established reputation. The vine-shaded setting is the restaurant's pièce de resistance.

9 Aimo e Nadia

MAP R2 ■ Via R Montecuccoli 6 ■ 02-416-886 ■ Closed Sat & Sun lunch, 3 wks Aug ■ €€€

Out in the suburbs, Aimo and Nadia (a Tuscan-born husband-and-wife team) run this place with exquisite taste throughout, and it ranks among Milan's very best *(see p66)*.

10 Cantina Piemontese

MAP N4 ■ Via Laghetto 2 ■ 02-7846-18 ■ Closed Aug ■ €€€

This small restaurant serves Piedmontese and Lombard fare. The vegetarian speciality is quiche with bean purée and artichokes.

Charming Cantina Piemontese

🔟 Lake Maggiore

The westernmost of Italy's great lakes straddles the Lombardy-Piedmont border and pokes its head into Switzerland. The southern half was, from the 15th century, a fiefdom of the powerful Borromeo clan. Maggiore's development as a holiday retreat for Europeans began in 1800 when Napoleon's Simplon highway from Geneva to Milan skirted its shores. Maggiore has fewer resorts than Garda and is not as breathtakingly pretty as Como, although the triplet Borromean Islands are stunning. Still, it avoids the over-development of Garda and the crowds of Como.

Garibaldi statue, Verbania

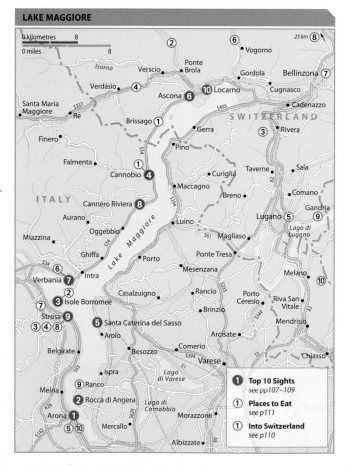

LAKE MAGGIORE

Top 10 Sights
see pp107–109

Places to Eat
see p111

Into Switzerland
see p110

1 Arona
MAP A3 ■ Tourist info: Piazzale Duca d'Aosta; 0322-243-601

This sprawling modern town was once a stronghold of the Borromeo family, but its fortress was razed by Napoleon. The only lasting monument to the great family is an enormous 17th-century bronze statue of San Carlo Borromeo. Clamber up a ladder-like stair to the head of the 23-m (75-ft) colossus to peek out through his pupils at the 17th-century church below. The road leading to this shrine was meant to be lined with 15 devotional chapels, but only two were finished.

2 Rocca di Angera
MAP A3 ■ Angera ■ 0331-931-300 ■ Open end Mar–end Oct: 9:30am–5:30pm daily (Oct: to 5pm) ■ Adm

This medieval castle, a Borromeo fortress since 1449, preserves a hall of crude frescoes which, dating from 1342–54, count among the oldest surviving Lombard-Gothic works on a non-religious subject. Wooden staircases lead to the tower and lake views. Most of the rooms now house a Doll Museum, with its splendid collection of Japanese figures and 18th- and 19th-century European examples.

3 Isole Borromee
MAP A2–A3

From the 1650s to today, the trio of tiny islands in the middle of Lake Maggiore has drawn admirers for the gracious palaces and ornate gardens built by the Borromeo family, who still own everything but the fishing village on Isola dei Pescatori. The islands are among Lombardy's top attractions (see pp30–31).

Arcaded street typical of Cannobio

4 Cannobio
MAP B2 ■ Tourist info: Via Antonio Giovanola 25; 0323-71-212; www.procannobio.it

By the Swiss border, at the foot of a rushing stream near the Orrido di Santa Anna gorge, Cannobio dates back more than 3,000 years, though its steep, crooked pebble lanes and faded buildings are mainly medieval. Restaurant tables line the harbour.

Borromean Isola Bella

Monastery of Santa Caterina del Sasso, on Maggiore's eastern shore

5 Santa Caterina del Sasso

MAP B3 ■ Outside Leggiuno
■ Open Apr–Oct: 9am–noon, 2–6pm daily (Mar: to 5pm; Nov–Feb: to 5pm Sat & Sun only)

In gratitude for being saved from a shipwreck, a 13th-century merchant built a chapel into the cliff face above the deepest part of the lake. There are some decaying frescoes, but the main attraction is the setting.

6 Ascona

MAP B2 ■ Tourist info: Via Papio 5; 0041-917-910-091; www. ascona-locarno.com

At the Swiss end of the lake, Ascona has been a favourite haunt of such cultural giants as Kandinsky, Freud and Thomas Mann. The town hosts a Harley rally and Jazz festival in July, and a Rolls-Royce gathering and classical music concerts in September. The streets are lined with top-end boutiques and sights such as the 16th-century church Santi Pietro e Paolo. Up on the mountainside is Monte Verità (Hill of Truth), which was established as a progressive colony in the early 20th century.

7 Verbania

MAP A2 ■ Tourist info: Via Ruga 44; 0323-556-669

In 1939 Mussolini gave the ancient Roman name "Verbania" to a group of villages here that include little Suna, industrialized Intra, and Pallanza, an important town in the Middle Ages. Pallanza's main sight is the landscaped garden of Villa Taranto (see p46), while its Palazzo Viani-Dugnani houses a collection of landscape paintings.

8 Cannero Riviera

MAP B2 ■ Tourist info: Via Angelo Orsi 1; 0323-788-943

Despite its northern locale, this sheltered promontory has a truly Mediterranean clime, enabling citrus trees and camellias to flourish. The lake vistas, steep medieval streets and 18th-century houses give it a

---

LAKE MAGGIORE EXPRESS

Spend one or two days seeing the best that the Lake Maggiore area has to offer. Crossing from Italy to Switzerland, the route consists of a boat trip on the lake and a ride on the exhilarating Centovalli railway through mountain scenery with unlimited stops along the way. Visit www.lagomaggioreexpress.eu.

pleasant feel. Most striking are the scraps of islands just offshore, sprouting glowering castles built by lake pirates in the 1400s and later used by the Borromeo clan as a defensive line against the Swiss.

⑨ Stresa

MAP A3 ■ Tourist info: 0323-301-50; www.parcozoopallavicino.it

The gateway to the Isole Borromee *(see pp30–31)* is a pretty lakeside town that offers hotels, a grid of trattoria-lined pedestrian streets and a summer music festival *(see p77)*. Just south of the town, the Villa Pallavicino has a botanical garden and a small zoo.

Stresa's lakeside promenade

⑩ Locarno

MAP B1 ■ Tourist info: in the Casino on Piazza Grande; 0041-917-910-091

Most of this city at the northern end of the lake was rebuilt along modern Swiss lines of concrete, glass and steel. What remains of the medieval city, however, is worth crossing the border for. The 14th-century Castello Visconteo is a highlight, as is the Santuario della Madonna del Sasso (1497), which has paintings by Ciseri and Bramantino (visit by cable-car). Artists Hans and Marguerite Arps donated many works to a modern art gallery in the lovely Casa Rusca.

A DAY ON LAKE MAGGIORE

▶ MORNING

Be at the **Stresa** ferry dock by 10am and buy a day pass for island-hopping as well as your admission tickets for the **Isole Borromee** *(see pp30–31)*.

Travel first to **Isola Bella** to spend a couple of hours exploring the collections of the **Borromeo Palace** and the intricate gardens above it. Then catch the 12:25pm ferry for the short hop to the **Isola dei Pescatori**, where you can settle at a lakeside table on **Verbano's** terrace for lunch with a view (book ahead, *see p111*).

MID-AFTERNOON

Wander the tourist/fishing village after lunch before continuing on the boat to **Isola Madre**.

The **Villa Borromeo** on Madre takes only 30 minutes to wander through, but the vast botanical gardens surrounding it are a delight, thick with exotic flora and populated by colourful exotic birds. The multilingual map handed out explains many of the rare specimens and is remarkably informative.

Try to catch a return ferry that stops on the mainland at Lido/Funivia for **Mottarone** – one stop before Stresa itself. Get off here and stroll along the little-used waterfront promenade for the final 20-minute walk back to downtown Stresa. You will be rewarded with a lovely late afternoon view of the islands on your left, and romantically crumbling, abandoned villas on your right.

See map on p106

Into Switzerland

 Brissago
MAP B2 ■ www.brissago.ch

Famous for its botanical gardens and two pretty islands, every summer Brissago hosts the JazzAscona festival, where artists perform on stages along the promenade.

2 Valle Maggia
MAP B1 ■ www.vallemaggia.ch

Just outside Locarno, Valle Maggia offers a network of valleys leading up to unspoiled Alpine peaks which are perfect for walks or rides.

3 Santa Maria degli Angeli, Monte Tamaro
MAP B2 ■ www.montetamaro.ch

At the top of the lake, cable-cars rise up to Monte Tamaro, offering great views. Here stands Mario Botta's Santa Maria degli Angeli (1997), an intimate memorial chapel.

 Centovalli Railway
www.centovalli.ch

This railway line runs from Locarno (see p109), through narrow valleys and over ancient bridges, to Domodossola in Italy. It's part of the Lago Maggiore Express (see p108).

5 Lugano
MAP B2 ■ www.lugano-tourism.ch

This chic city, the halfway point between Lakes Maggiore and Como, sits on its own lake. It has a historic centre and a lakeside promenade.

 Verzasca Valley
MAP B1 ■ www.verzasca.net

You can swim in a jade-green lake and explore the tiny hamlets of this pretty valley. Hundreds of trails include high-mountain hikes that cross peaks, passes and pastures.

 Bellinzona
MAP C1 ■ www.bellinzona turismo.ch

Low-key Bellinzona is home to fine architecture and a stupendous trio of castles granted UNESCO World Heritage Site status in 2000.

 Alto Ticino
MAP C1 ■ www.ticino.ch

The Alto Ticino, a place of lonesome valleys and soaring skies, has two ancient passes – San Gottardo and San Bernardino – that linked north and south Europe in times past.

9 Gandria
MAP C2

A romantic hideaway east along the lake from Lugano, Gandria tumbles down the hillside to the water's edge. Terrace cafés offer idyllic views.

10 Monte Generoso
MAP C2 ■ www.monte generoso.ch

Capolago is the access point for the rack railway up Monte Generoso (1,705 m/5,595 ft). The panorama takes in Milan and Turin as well as Lakes Como and Maggiore.

Lake Lugano, viewed from one of its magnificent surrounding peaks

Places to Eat

Dining at dusk at Lo Scalo, Cannobio

① Lo Scalo, Cannobio
MAP B2 ■ Piazza Vittorio Emanuele II 32 ■ 0323-71-480 ■ Closed Mon ■ €€€

The best of Cannobio's restaurants offers traditional Piedmontese cooking with inventive touches.

② Verbano, Isola dei Pescatori
MAP A3 ■ 0323-32-534 ■ Closed Nov–Mar ■ €€€

Set on a terrace at the tip of the island, with great views of Isola Bella. The fish is superb.

③ Piemontese, Stresa
MAP A3 ■ Via Mazzini 25 ■ 0323-30-235 ■ Closed Mon & Dec–Jan ■ €€

Enjoy local dishes in the wood-panelled dining room and cobbled courtyard of Stresa's top restaurant.

④ Il Vicoletto, Stresa
MAP A3 ■ Vicolo del Poncivo 3 ■ 0323-932-102 ■ Closed Thu (except Mar–Oct) & mid-Jan–mid-Feb ■ €€€

Homemade pasta, tasty risotto and fish from the lake, a good selection of wines and a few veranda tables.

⑤ La Vecchia Arona, Arona
MAP A3 ■ Via Lungolago Marconi 17 ■ 0322-242-469 ■ Closed Wed ■ €€

Franco Carrera is an enthusiastic and innovative reinterpreter of "traditional" dishes. Book ahead.

⑥ Milano, Pallanza
MAP A2 ■ Corso Zanitello 2 ■ 0323-556-816 ■ Closed Tue & mid-Nov–Feb ■ €€

Verbania's best restaurant serves classic Piedmontese dishes and lake fish in lovely grounds.

⑦ La Rampolina, Campino
MAP A3 ■ Via Someraro 13 ■ 0323-923-415 ■ Closed Mon ■ €€

On a hillside above Stresa, there are lovely lake views from the wisteria-canopied terrace. Local mountain cheeses feature on a tempting menu which also includes several lake-fish specialities.

⑧ Osteria degli Amici, Stresa
MAP A3 ■ Via Bolongaro 31 ■ 0323-30-453 ■ Closed mid-Nov–early Feb ■ €€

This convivial spot has some outdoor tables and a menu ranging from pizza to freshly caught lake fish.

Appetizer at Verbano

⑨ Il Sole di Ranco
MAP A3 ■ Piazza Venezia 5 ■ 0331-976-507 ■ Closed Mon lunch, Tue lunch & Christmas–Feb ■ €€€

Historic Il Sole offers a fresh take on Italian regional cuisine (see p67).

⑩ Enoteca Il Grappolo, Arona
MAP A3 ■ Via Pertossi 7 ■ 0322-47735 ■ Closed weekday lunch & Tue ■ €€

This wine bar's menu usually includes platters of local meats and cheeses, polenta and high-quality Piedmont beef, with wine-pairing recommendations for each dish.

See map on p106

🔟 Lake Como

Interior of the Basilica in Como

Como is the beauty queen of the Italian lakes, the turquoise and sapphire waters of its three arms – 50 km (30 miles) long, but rarely more than 2 km (1 mile) wide – are backed by the snow-capped peaks of the pre-Alps. Its diversity runs from windsurfing and Alpine vistas in the north to the busy towns capping the southern arms, such as Como, a Roman city with a glorious cathedral and silk industry, and Lecco, full of literary associations. For centuries Lake Como has drawn in the wealthy to line its shores with gracious villas and verdant gardens; it has also inspired composers (Liszt, Verdi, Bellini) and writers such as Byron, Shelley and Wordsworth.

LAKE COMO

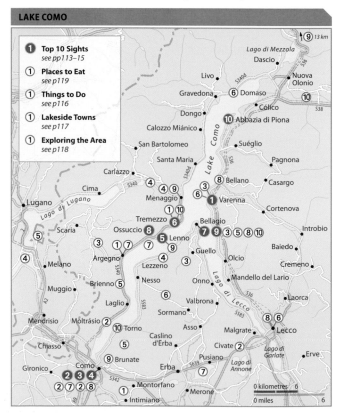

Top 10 Sights
see pp113–15

Places to Eat
see p119

Things to Do
see p116

Lakeside Towns
see p117

Exploring the Area
see p118

Lake Como viewed from the loggia of Villa Monastero, Varenna

1 Villa Monastero, Varenna

MAP C2 ▪ Via Polvani 2 ▪ Open Mar–Sep: 9am–6:30pm daily; Jan–Feb: 11am–5pm Sun ▪ Adm ▪ www.villa monastero.eu

This villa – a former convent – has gardens that stretch right down to the lakeshore, wonderfully shaded throughout by the canopies of cypresses and palms (see p46).

2 Basilica di Sant'Abbondio, Como

MAP C3 ▪ Via Sant'Abbondio (off Viale Innocenzo XI) ▪ Open 8am–6pm daily (to 4:30pm in winter)

In Como's industrial suburbs, this Romanesque church retains a pair of bell towers and an extended choir that links it, architecturally, to the Westwerk style of medieval Germany. The apse is gorgeously frescoed with a series of biblical scenes.

3 Brunate Funicular, Como

MAP C3 ▪ Piazza A De Gasperi ▪ 031-303-608 ▪ Runs every 30 mins 6am–10:30pm daily (to midnight Sat in summer) ▪ Adm

The classic journey to this hillside village is to take a short walk from Como's harbour to the funicular station, then ride the funicular up to Brunate. You're rewarded with vistas over Como and the lake, and this is also the starting point of many trails into the surrounding hills.

4 Duomo, Como

MAP C3 ▪ Piazza del Duomo ▪ 031-265-244 ▪ Open 7am–7pm

Como's cathedral was begun in 1396, but not capped with its dome until 1740. The façade's pilasters are lined with saints, and the main door is flanked by the figures of two local ancient scholars, the Plinys, Elder and Younger. Inside there are fine tapestries and an intricately carved and painted altarpiece of 1492.

Vaulted ceilings of Como's Duomo

Statues at Villa Balbianello

5 Villa Balbianello, Lenno
MAP C2 ■ Lenno ■ 0344-56-110
■ Open Mid-Mar–mid-Nov: 10am–6pm Tue, Thu–Sun ■ Adm

The slender twin turrets and the statue-lined balustrades that outline the terraced gardens of this 1784 villa have caught the eye of many a film director. Head to the villa by boat from Lenno and then proceed on foot. To tour the villa itself, it is essential to book in advance (see p46).

6 Villa Carlotta, Tremezzo
MAP C2 ■ Tremezzo ■ 0344-40-405 ■ Open mid-Mar–1 Nov 9:30am–5pm; Apr–Oct: to 7:30pm (Jun–Jul: to 9pm Tue); Nov: 10am– 4:30pm Sat & Sun ■ Adm ■ www.villacarlotta.it

This is one of the lake's sumptuous villas, with exquisitely landscaped gardens. Unusually, you can tour the art-strewn villa here, as well as its wonderful surrounds (see p47).

7 Villa Serbelloni, Bellagio
MAP C2 ■ Piazza della Chiesa, Bellagio ■ 031-951-555 ■ Tours mid-Mar–mid-Nov: 11am and 3:30pm Tue–Sun ■ Adm ■ www.villa serbelloni.com

Bellagio's promontory has been prime real estate for millennia. Pliny the Younger had a villa named "Tragedy" here (it was paired with a "Comedy" villa on the far shore), which was replaced by a castle in the Middle Ages, then a Stagna family villa in the 15th century. The last Stagna left it to his best friend Serbelloni in 1788. Serbelloni proceeded to rebuild the villa as a summer residence to the main house down in the village (now Grand Hotel Villa Serbelloni). In 1959, the summer home passed to the Rockefeller Foundation, and now visiting scholars can live and study here for short periods. It is not open to the public, but you can tour the gardens (see p47).

8 Sacro Monte di Ossuccio
MAP C2 ■ Madonna del Soccorso: open Mar–Oct: 7am–7pm daily; www.sacrimonti.net

This series of 15 chapels standing in a panoramic position on the hillside behind Ossuccio is one of nine such sites in northern Italy, constructed in the 16th and 17th centuries to convey the teachings of the Catholic church

Villa Carlotta, Tremezzo

with frescoes and life-size statues. Here there are 230, made of terracotta and plaster. The final chapel is within the Madonna del Soccorso church.

9 Villa Melzi, Bellagio
MAP C2 ■ Lungolario Manzoni ■ 031-950-204 ■ Open end Mar–Oct: 9:30am–6:30pm daily ■ Adm ■ www.giardinidivillamelzi.it

The manicured gardens surrounding the elegant Neo-Classical home of Francesco Melzi d'Eril, Napoleon's man in Italy, are now open to the public (see p47).

Moorish temple folly at Villa Melzi

10 Abbazia di Piona
MAP C2 ■ Signposted off the lake road ■ 0341-940-331 ■ Open 9am–noon, 2:30–6pm daily

At the tip of the Ogliasca peninsula sits this Benedictine abbey, cloaked in silence. The abbey was founded in the 9th century, and the little church has Romanesque carvings decorating the water stoups and the capitals and bases of the columns in the quiet cloister. The monks distill – and sell – some potent liqueurs.

COMO SILK

Como has been Italy's silk capital since 1510. While they now import the spun thread from China, the fabrics Como's artisans weave is still the most sought after by Milan's top designers. There are shops and warehouse stores all around town hawking silk wares. In the city outskirts, there is even a Museum of Silk (Via Castelnuovo 9; 031-303-180; www.museosetacomo.com).

COMO LAKE-HOPPING

▶ MORNING

To cruise the lake you can buy point-to-point tickets, or consider the single-ticket cruises that visit several towns and may include villa admissions. This itinerary assumes you have checked out Como's sights before spending the night in **Bellagio** (see p117).

Begin the next day with a cappuccino at Bellagio's Caffè Rossi across from the dock before boarding the 10:30am boat to **Villa Carlotta**, where you have an hour to visit the collection of art and lush gardens of the lake's greatest villa.

Afterwards, catch the ferry down to **Isola Comacina** to dig into a sumptuous feast at the **Locanda** (see p119). After a second helping of their "spiked" coffee, you'll have a bit of time to work off the meal by exploring the island's overgrown church ruins before grabbing the boat back up the lake to **Varenna** (see p117).

MID-AFTERNOON

Continue walking off your indulgent lunch by climbing up to the romantic, panoramic Castello di Vezio above the town, then descend and pop into some of Varenna's little churches. Poke around the gardens of **Villa Monastero** (see p113), then finally head down to the lakefront arcade for a short stroll then a meal by the water at **Vecchia Varenna** (see p119).

Unless you decide to spend a relaxing night in quiet and little-visited Varenna, make sure you finish dinner before 9pm, when the last ferry leaves for Bellagio.

See map on p112 ←

Things to Do

1 Playing a Round of Golf
Circolo Villa d'Este, Montorfano:
031-200-200 ▪ Golf Club Menaggio &
Cadenabbia: 0344-32-103; www.
menaggio.org

If you have a handicap of 36 or less,
try for a reservation at the Circolo
Villa d'Este and check out the course
of Golf Club Menaggio & Cadenabbia.

2 Hiring a Motorboat
Boat hire, Moltrasio: www.
nettunonoleggiobarche.it ▪ Boat hire
& taxi-boats, Cernobbio: www.taxi
boatcernobbio.it

Motorboats are available for hire with
or without a licence in many places
around the lake, or you can sit back
and relax with a private taxi-boat.

3 Mountain Biking
Bike hire: Comolagobike:
www.comolagobike.com

The hills of Bellagio's peninsula are
great mountain-bike country.

Mountain biking on a forest trail

4 Horse Riding
Trekking centre: Maneggio dei
Tre Laghi; 392-032-2903

Choose an English- or Western-style
saddle and trek mountain valleys off
the Menaggio–Porlezza Road.

5 Climbing
Info at CAI, Via Papa Giovanni
XXIII, Lecco; www.cai.lecco.it

You can rock-climb in the mountains
ringing the lake's southeastern end.

Windsurfing on the lake

6 Windsurfing
Windsurfcenter Domaso: 380-
700-0010; www.wsc-domaso.com
▪ Fun Surf Centre, Dervio: 338-814-
8719; www.funsurfcentre.com

The strong winds of the lake's
northern end draw an international
crowd of windsurfers.

7 Flying by Seaplane
Aero Club Como: www.
aeroclubcomo.com

Take a bird's-eye view of the lake and
alight on water for an unforgettable
experience. The pilots at the Aero
Club Como are highly professional.

8 Kayaking
Boat hire: Cavalcalario Club,
Gallasco; 3395-308-138 ▪ Società
Canottieri, Via Nullo 2, Lecco; 0341-
364-273; www.canottieri.lecco.it

Get a deliciously different perspective
on Como's fabled coastline, peeking
into private lakeside gardens from
your own kayak or canoe.

9 Hiking
There's plenty of choice for
walkers around Lake Como including
signposted trails from the Brunate
funicular (see p113) and the Greenway
between Colonno and Cadenabbia.

10 Lake Cruises
Bellagio: www.bellagiowater
limousines.com ▪ Menaggio: www.
menaggiowatertaxi.com

Small-group boat tours from Bellagio
can include a visit to Villa Balbianello
(see p113) and sunset tours, with
Prosecco, run daily from Menaggio.

→ *See map on p112*

Lakeside Towns

1 Tremezzo
MAP C2 ▪ Tourist info: IAT, Via Regina 3; 0344-404-93

A tiny resort whose main claim to fame is the Villa Carlotta (see p114).

2 Como
MAP C3 ▪ Tourist info: Via Pretorio; 031-304-137; www.lakecomo.org ▪ Local info: near railway station S. Giovanni; 3420-076-403

Italy's silk capital was founded by the Romans and has a spectacular cathedral (see p113), a handful of modest museums, lots of boutiques and two ancient churches.

3 Varenna
MAP C2 ▪ Info at Via IV Novembre 7; 0341-830-367

Arguably, Varenna makes a better base for exploring the lake than busy Bellagio (see p51).

4 Menaggio
MAP C2 ▪ Tourist info: Piazza Garibaldi 8; 0344-32-924

This is a pleasant little resort on the main ferry lines, with some Baroque churches and a pretty promenade.

5 Bellagio
MAP C2 ▪ Info at ferry dock on Piazza Mazzini; 031-950-204; www.bellagiolakecomo.com

A popular town, with the gardens of villas Serbelloni and Melzi (see pp114–15), a Romanesque church, a café-lined harbourfront and a pretty warren of medieval alleys.

6 Lecco
MAP D3 ▪ Info at Piazza XX Settembre 23; 0341-295-720; www.lakecomo.com

The capital of the lake's southeastern arm is famous for sights linked to native writer Alessandro Manzoni, who set parts of his *I Promessi Sposi* (see p52) in the suburb of Olate.

7 Argegno
MAP C2

A picturesque marina. Take the cable-car up to Pigra for wonderful views or follow the road inland to explore the lovely Val Intelvi (see p118).

8 Bellano
MAP C2 ▪ Info at railway station; 335-175-2102

On Piazza S Giorgio sits the black-and-white striped façade of Santi Nazaro e Celso. A steep street leads to the entrance of the dramatic Orrido gorge, which can be explored.

9 Lenno
MAP C2 ▪ Info at Piazza XI Febbraio; 0344-558-3417 (Sat–Mon)

Don't miss the 11th-century Santo Stefano and neighbouring baptistry. Just north of town, in Mezzegra, a black cross marks where Mussolini was shot by partisans.

10 Torno
MAP C3

This pretty village features a lakeside piazza and a miniscule marina. The medieval church has a narrow bell tower and striking decorated interior.

Bellagio's peninsula viewed from the lake

Exploring the Area

 Bikesharing
bicincitta.tobike.it
There are about a dozen bike-sharing points around Como, including at the main San Giovanni railway station and at Tavernola, near Cernobbio.

 Civate, Lake Annone
MAP C3 ■ San Pietro al Monte: www.amicidisanpietro.it
On the shores of Lake Annone, Civate is the starting point for walks up to the attractive monastic complex of San Pietro al Monte which has stunning frescoes.

Fresco at San Pietro al Monte near Civate

 **Valle Intelvi**
MAP C2 ■ Valle Intelvi Tourist Board: www.valleintelviturismo.it
Stretching from Argegno (see p117) up to Lanzo d'Intelvi, this scenic valley is flanked by wooded hillsides dotted with ancient villages (see p59).

4 **Lake Lugano**
MAP B2-C2 ■ Lugano Tourist Board: www.luganoturismo.ch
It's a 12-km (7-mile) drive from Menaggio (see p117) to attractive Lake Lugano, which spans the Italian-Swiss border, and the pretty town of Lugano itself (see p110).

5 **Campione d'Italia**
MAP C2 ■ Campione d'Italia Tourist Board: www.campione italia.com
An Italian enclave, Campione d'Italia has a lovely setting on Lake Lugano. Steps zig-zag from the lake to the Santuario della Madonna dei Ghirli church, with a fine frescoed interior.

6 **Pian del Tivano**
MAP C2
The panoramic road inland from the lakeside village of Nesso leads to this grassy plateau. It's a popular place for picnics and walking.

7 **Lago di Pusiano**
MAP C3 ■ Boat schedules vary, www.prolocobosisio.it
This is one of several smaller lakes between the lower branches of Lake Como. Eco-friendly boat tours are organized in summer.

8 **Vehicle Hire**
Barindelli Tourist Board: www.barindelli.it
As well as providing chauffeured services and private transfers, Barindelli also rents cars and scooters: an ideal way to explore the area.

9 **Chiavenna**
MAP D1
The charming historic town of Chiavenna is famous for its *crotti* – natural caves used as cellars for storing wine, salami and cheese; many are now restaurants that are wonderful to visit in both summer and winter.

10 **Valtellina**
MAP D1 ■ Valtellina Tourist Board: www.valtellina.it
To the northeast of Lake Como, Valtellina is famous for its ski resorts. Bormio has a lovely historic centre, as excellent mountain food and robust red wines (see p59).

Valtellina ski resort cable-cars

Places to Eat

PRICE CATEGORIES

For a three-course meal for one with half a bottle of wine (or equivalent meal), taxes and extra charges.

€ under €35　€€ €35–€60　€€€ over €60

1 La P'Osteria, Argegno
MAP C2 ▪ Via Lungo Telo Sinistra 3 ▪ 031-447-4072 ▪ Closed Tue & Wed in winter ▪ €€

Contemporary versions of local dishes, game and quality meats from Piedmont are on the menu. The peaceful position by the river as it flows into the lake is a bonus.

2 Pronobis, Como
MAP C3 ▪ Via Lambertenghi 19 ▪ 031-261-786 ▪ Closed Sun (except Dec) ▪ €

This country-style deli-restaurant is ideal for lunch in central Como. Try the house meatloaf and homemade pear, walnut and chocolate dessert.

3 Barchetta, Bellagio
MAP C2 ▪ Salita Mella 13 ▪ 031-951-389 ▪ Closed Tue (except Jul & Aug) & Nov–Easter ▪ €€€

For a beloved resort, Bellagio oddly lacks superlative eateries, save perhaps this "little boat". Dishes are well-made, the ambience amicable and the prices reasonable (see p67).

4 Ittiturismo Da Abate, Lezzeno
MAP C2 ▪ Frazione Villa 4 ▪ 031-914-986 ▪ Closed lunch & Mon ▪ €

Run by a family of fishermen who will happily show you how the fish is caught and prepared. Try the pasta with lake-fish ragout or *fritto misto*.

5 Crotto dei Platani, Brienno
MAP C2 ▪ Via Regina 73 ▪ 031-814-038 ▪ €€€

This restaurant is set in a lakeside grotto, with a gorgeous terrace right on the water, and serves regional food with an inventive touch.

6 Vecchia Varenna, Varenna
MAP C2 ▪ Contrada Scoscesa 14 ▪ 0341-830-793 ▪ Closed Mon in winter, Dec & Jan ▪ €€

Within a 15th-century building, the most romantic restaurant on the lake serves creative local cuisine.

Locanda dell'Isola's outdoor tables

7 Locanda dell'Isola Comacina, Ossuccio
MAP C2 ▪ Isola Comacina ▪ 0344-55-083 ▪ No credit cards ▪ Closed Nov–Mar; mid-Mar–mid-Jun: Tue ▪ €€€

The fixed-price feast has stayed the same since 1947: antipasto, trout, chicken, cheese, fruit, gelato, water, wine and brandy-spiked coffee.

8 Osteria del Gallo, Como
MAP C3 ▪ Via Vitani 16 ▪ 031-272-591 ▪ Closed Mon eve, Sun ▪ €

A popular, family-run eatery in Como's historic centre. The menu changes daily but often includes lentil and spelt soup or polenta.

9 Bar Costantin – La Trattoria
MAP C2 ▪ Via Camozzi 16, Menaggio ▪ 0344-31000 ▪ €

This family-run trattoria offers home cooked lake fish, regional dishes and a good selection of pizzas.

10 La Fagurida, Tremezzina
MAP C2 ▪ Via Rogaro 17 ▪ 0344-40676 ▪ Closed Mon, Jan & Feb ▪ €€

A charming trattoria in the hills, with lake views. Come for tasty homecooking and seasonal dishes.

See map on p112

TOP **Lake Garda**

Lake Garda is an area of contrasts. The crosswinds to the north and the dominating slopes of Monte Baldo draw windsurfers and paragliders, while to the south the edges of the lake are gentler, with stony beaches, and lemon and olive groves in the vine-covered hills. Garda also has some of the best Roman-era remains in northern Italy at Sirmione and Desenzano, as well as medieval castles in Torri del Benaco, Malcesine, Valeggio and Sirmione. It is the largest of the main Italian lakes, with a milder, more Mediterranean temperature than might be expected for its latitude. As a result, Lake Garda is the most-visited of the Italian lakes.

Fountain at Il Vittoriale

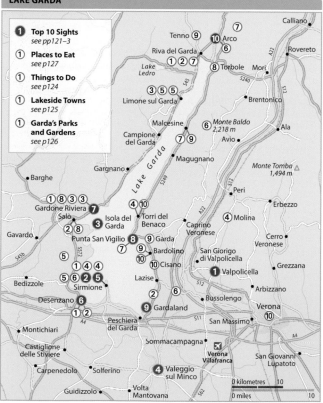

LAKE GARDA

1 Top 10 Sights
see pp121–3

1 Places to Eat
see p127

1 Things to Do
see p124

1 Lakeside Towns
see p125

1 Garda's Parks and Gardens
see p126

0 kilometres 10
0 miles 10

1 Valpolicella

MAP G4 ■ Tourist info: www.valpolicellaweb.it; www.stradadelvino valpolicella.it ■ Winery tour: www.seregoalighieri.it

Nestled between Lake Garda and Verona, Valpolicella has been a renowned wine-making area since ancient Roman times. Nowadays it's particularly famous for its reds – the complex and heady Amarone, made using air-dried grapes, as well as Valpolicella. Among the villages, hillside San Giorgio is one to see, while Serego-Alighieri, owned by descendants of medieval poet Dante, offers an interesting winery tour.

2 Grotte di Catullo, Sirmione

MAP G4 ■ Via Catullo ■ 030-916-157 ■ Open 8:30am–7pm Tue–Sun (to 6:30pm Sun); winter: 8:30am–4:30pm (to 2pm Sun) ■ Adm

Though the ancient Roman poet Catullus did take his holidays at Sirmione, there's no evidence to suggest that this ancient house at the very tip of Sirmione's peninsula was actually his villa – in fact, it was probably built after Catullus's death, sometime in the 1st century BC. It is the best surviving example of a Roman private home in northern Italy, but this didn't stop it being misnamed a "grotto", the result of the romantically over-grown and cavelike state it had assumed by the Middle Ages.

3 Isola del Garda

MAP G4 ■ Boats from Barbarano and Gardone ■ 328-612-6943 ■ Tours: Apr–Oct: Tue & Thu at 9:30am ■ Adm (book in advance) ■ www.isoladelgarda.com

Garda's largest island once housed a monastery that attracted the great medieval saints: Francis of Assisi, Anthony of Padua and Bernardino of Siena. It was destroyed by Napoleon and replaced in 1890–1903 with a Neo-Gothic Venetian-style villa and luxuriant gardens. Guided tours include a boat ride and a snack.

Aerial view of lovely Isola del Garda

4 Giardino Sigurtà

MAP G5 ■ Via Cavour 1, Valeggio sul Mincio ■ 045-637-1033 ■ Open Apr–Nov: 9am–7pm daily; Mar, Oct & Nov: to 6pm ■ Adm ■ www.sigurta.it

Carlo Sigurtà spent 40 years turning a barren hillside into one of Italy's great gardens, with manicured lawns and pathways amid vibrant flower-beds and reflecting pools. It's a 20-minute drive south of the lakeside.

Grotte di Catullo, Sirmione

Dramatic fortress of Rocca Scaligera on Sirmione's peninsula

5 Rocca Scaligera, Sirmione

MAP G4 ▪ Piazza Castello ▪ 030-916-468 ▪ Open 8:30am–7pm Tue–Sun (to 1pm Sun) ▪ Adm

At the narrowest point of Sirmione's long, thin peninsula, this striking, pale-grey stone citadel, in use as a fortress until the 19th century, still guards the town – the only way to enter Sirmione is via drawbridge over the moat. It's worth climbing the 30-m (95-ft) tower for the grand panorama.

6 Villa Romana, Desenzano

Mosaic floor at Villa Romana

MAP G4 ▪ Via Crocefisso 22 ▪ 030-914-3547 ▪ Open 8:30am–7pm Tue–Sun; Nov–Feb : to 5pm ▪ Adm

The most important late Imperial villa remaining in Northern Italy was built in the 1st century BC, but the fine polychrome floor mosaics are mostly of the 4th and 5th centuries. By that time, the local Romans were Christianized, which explains the late 4th-century glass bowl engraved with an image of Christ.

7 Giardino Botanico Hruska, Gardone Riviera

MAP G4 ▪ Gardone Riviera ▪ Tourist info: IAT Gardone; 030-374-8736 ▪ Open Mar–Oct: 9am– 7pm daily ▪ Adm ▪ www. hellergarden.com

This lovely set of botanical gardens features more than 2,000 Alpine species on its terraced hillside (see p47).

8 Punta San Vigilio

MAP G4 ▪ Tourist info: www. punta-sanvigilio.it

This is an idyllic little promontory jutting out into Lake Garda, with lemon and olive groves, café tables around an enchanting port, and an exclusive hotel. The Parlo Baia della Sirene (Mermaid's Beach) has an inviting beach club fringed by olive trees, which charges for entry in the day-time but offers activities for children. In the early evenings the beach is free, and it's the perfect place to watch the sun go down (see p126).

LAKESIDE BATTLES

In the 13th–15th centuries Venice vied with Milan for control of Lombardy (see p38). The town of Torbole (see p125) was the scene of a historic Milanese victory in 1439. Venice was caught trying to smuggle supplies to the town of Brescia – 26 ships had been sailed up the Adige River and dragged overland via Torbole into the lake.

9 Gardaland

MAP G4 ■ On the shore road, north of Peschiera ■ 045-644-9777 ■ Closed Nov–Mar (except Christmas–New Year) ■ Adm ■ www.gardaland.it

Under the icon of a green dragon named Prezzemolo ("Parsley"), the park boasts roller coasters and carnival rides, a water park, jungle safari, ice shows, dolphin tricks and medieval spectacles. Italy's greatest theme park is a hoot for the kids (see p60).

10 Castello di Arco, near Riva

MAP H2 ■ 0464-510-156 ■ Open daily Apr–Sep: 10am–7pm; Mar & Oct: 10am–5pm; Nov–Feb 10am–4pm; Jan: 10am–4pm Sat & Sun only (last adm 1 hr before closing) ■ Adm

This 12th-century castle is in near-total ruin. Only one wall remains of the central keep, and the sole room in the whole complex to survive intact was filled with debris until 1986. When it was cleared, a number of excellent 14th-century frescoes were found, depicting nobles playing at board games and war.

Magnificent ruins of Castello di Arco

TWO DAYS ON LAKE GARDA

Malcesine · Monte Baldo

Punta San Vigilio

Sirmione · Cantina Fratelli Zeni · Olive Oil Museum

Desenzano

Peschiera del Garda

▷ DAY ONE

If you're here to relax and sightsee rather than thrash up the waves near Riva (see p125), then spend your days exploring the southern end of the lake. **Sirmione** (see p125) is both a charming and lively base.

On your first day, spend time in **Desenzano** (see p125) to see the **Villa Romana** before driving out to Sirmione itself. Walk out to the far tip of the peninsula to wander the ruins of the **Grotte di Catullo** (see p121). On your way back into town, divert to the right to pop into San Pietro and see its medieval frescoes.

Navigate the throngs of the tiny centre to climb the balustrades of the **Rocca Scaligera** for a sunset panorama.

Stroll through Sirmione's historic centre, ending up at **Trattoria La Fiasca** (see p127) for a delicious lake-fish dinner.

DAY TWO

Set off along the lake's east coast, stopping, soon after pretty Lazise, to visit the free **Olive Oil Museum** (see p124) in Cisano and **Cantina Fratelli Zeni** (see p124) just beyond, for their wine museum and wine-tasting. Make **Punta San Vigilio** your lunchtime break, at a tavern table by the harbour or under the olive trees.

Unless you opt to stay here for an afternoon at the beach, carry on to **Malcesine** (see p125), to see the castle and take the cable-car up **Monte Baldo** (see p124) for some breathtaking panoramic views.

See map on p120 ←

Things to Do

 Windsurfing
Windsurfers flock to Garda's wind-pounded northern shores, especially Riva and Torbole, for some of Europe's best lake surfing.

2 **Diving**
While this isn't the tropics, the lake's waters are clearer than you might expect. Sights worth seeing include an underwater Jesus near Riva. Equipment is widely available.

3 **Mountain-Biking**
Explore the flatlands to the south, tackle mountains rising sheer from the north shores, or simply wend along the lake shore itself.

 Swimming
Garda's beaches are rocky, but the water is crystal clear. The best are at Sirmione, including Spiaggia Giamaica at the end of the peninsula.

Lake-swimming near Sirmione

 Golfing
MAP G4 ■ Gardagolf: Soiano del Lago; www.gardagolf.it ■ Arganza Golf Club: Calvagese della Riviera; www.arzagagolf.it
Garda is one of Italy's premier golf destinations, with ten clubs on the southern shore including two 27-hole courses, named Gardagolf and Arzaga.

 Monte Baldo Cable-Car
MAP H3 ■ Cable-car: www.funiviadelbaldo.it
Panoramic revolving pods take 20 minutes to ascend from Malcesine for walking and mountain-biking trails, paragliding and skiing.

Alpine Climbing near Lake Garda

7 **Climbing and Paragliding**
MAP H2-H3 ■ Guide Alpine: www.guidealpinearco.com ■ Climbing Stadium Rockmaster: 334-773-4133 ■ Paragliding Club: www.paraglidingmalcesine.it
Head to Arco for Guide Alpine and Multi Sport Centre for climbing, or to Malcesine for its Paragliding Club.

8 **Kayaking and SUP**
Kayaks and SUPs (stand-up-paddleboards) make it possible to explore inlets and bays not always accessible from dry land.

9 **Wine-Tasting**
MAP G4 ■ Cantina Fratelli Zeni, Bardolino; www.museodelvino.it
Some excellent wines are made on Lake Garda (see p65). Local wineries offer tastings, and Cantina Fratelli Zeni also has a wine museum.

10 **Olive Oil Museum**
MAP G4 ■ Via Peschiera 54, Cisano di Bardolino ■ Open 9:30am–12:30pm, 2:30–7pm Mon–Sat, 9am–noon Sun (booking required, email: info@museo.com)
This free museum gives a fascinating insight into the history of olive oil, one of Lake Garda's prime products. There's an actual waterwheel in action, and huge wooden oil presses.

Lakeside Towns

1 **Desenzano**
MAP G4 ■ Tourist info: Via
Porto Vecchio 34; 030-374-8726
A large and delightful town, settled
in the Bronze Age and a retreat since
the Roman era. Its top attraction is
the Villa Romana *(see p122)*.

2 **Salò**
MAP G4 ■ Tourist info: Piazza
Sant'Antonio 4; 030-374-8745
This genteelly faded resort became
the capital of Mussolini's short-lived
Republic of Salò (1943–5) in the
closing chapters of World War II.

3 **Gardone Riviera**
MAP G4 ■ Tourist info: Corso
della Repubblica 1; 030-3748-736
Gardone has many magnificent villas
and gardens, including the Giardino
Botanico Hruska *(see p122)* and
d'Annunzio's Il Vittoriale *(see p126)*.

4 **Torri del Benaco**
MAP G4 ■ Tourist info: Viale
Gardesana; 045-629-6482
This little town was once the capital
of Lake Garda. There's a Scaglieri
castle with a modest museum, and a
trail leads up from the town to cliffs
bearing 8,000-year-old rock etchings.

5 **Limone sul Garda**
MAP G3 ■ Tourist info:
Via IV Novembre 29; 0365-918-987;
www.limonehotels.com
Limone is tucked in a cove, with
a long beach, small harbour and
dozens of hotels, most of which are
closed from November until Easter.

6 **Sirmione**
MAP G4 ■ Tourist info:
Viale Marconi 8; 030-916-114;
www.comune.sirmione.bs.it
The loveliest town on the lake is set
at the tip of a long peninsula. It has
the ruins of an ancient Roman villa
and a medieval castle *(see pp121–2)*.

7 **Riva del Garda**
MAP H3 ■ Tourist info: Largo
Medaglie d'Oro 5; 0464-554-444;
www.gardatrentinonline.it
A bustling town, with the medieval
Torre d'Apponale and Rocca Castle.
Just inland lies Arco, home to a
ruined castle *(see p123)*.

8 **Torbole**
MAP H3 ■ Tourist info: Via
Lungolago Conca d'Oro 25; 0464-
505-177
History put Torbole on the map in
1439 *(see p122)*, but it's known chiefly
as a good base for windsurfing.

9 **Malcesine**
MAP H3 ■ Tourist info: Via
Gardesana 238; 0457-400-044
The town's castle contains a room
devoted to Goethe, who was briefly
suspected of being a spy when he
was seen sketching the castle.

10 **Bardolino**
MAP G4 ■ Tourist info: Piazzale
Aldo Moro 5; 045-721-0078
Bardolino has been famous since
Roman times for its light red wine.
The town also has two wonderful
Romanesque churches.

View over Limone sul Garda

Garda's Parks and Gardens

Streams and lakes of Heller Garden

1 Heller Garden, Gardone
MAP G4 ■ Via Roma 2
■ 336-410-887 ■ Adm ■ www.heller garden.it

This oasis of bamboo forest and water features was created in 1901, and is now owned by the artist André Heller, who has added works by the likes of Roy Lichtenstein and Keith Haring.

2 Aqua Paradise, Garda
MAP G4 ■ Fossalta 1 ■ 045-696-9900 ■ Adm ■ www.caneva world.it

This extensive water park is a family favourite for its range of waterslides, thrilling rapids and soaking rides.

3 Limonaia
MAP G3 ■ www.comune. limonesulgarda.bs.it

These elaborate, greenhouse-like "lemon houses" have been built since the 1200s to protect Garda's famed lemons from the elements. You can visit the elegant Limonaia del Castèl.

4 Parco delle Cascate di Molina
MAP H4 ■ Località Vaccarole, 37022 Molina, Fumane VR ■ Adm ■ www.parcodellecascate.it

Hiking paths lead to spectacular waterfalls at this little-known park.

5 Olive Groves, Sirmione
Olive groves line the route to the Grotte di Catullo (see p121).

6 Public Garden, Arco
MAP H2 ■ Viale delle Palme

Opposite the casino in the heart of Arco is a beautiful public garden filled with exotic plants and palms.

7 Parco Baia delle Sirene, Punta San Vigilio
Siren's Bay on Punta San Vigilio is a pay beach, but it is a lovely spot set among olive groves (see p122).

8 Il Vittoriale, Gardone Riviera
MAP G4 ■ Il Vittoriale ■ 0365-296-511 ■ Adm ■ www.vittoriale.it

The eccentric, flamboyant Gabriele d'Annunzio (see p46) set out the terraced gardens that surround his Art Nouveau residence. There's an amphitheatre, and his mausoleum is at the highest point of the estate.

Villa and gardens of Il Vittoriale

9 Parco Grotta Cascata Varone, North of Riva
MAP H3 ■ Via Cascata 12, Tenno, Riva del Garda ■ 0464 521 421 ■ Adm ■ www.cascata-varone.com

Make your way over this spectacular gorge via a series of suspended walk-ways, with white water all around.

10 Giardino Giusti, Verona
MAP H4 ■ Adm ■ www. tourism.verona.it

These formal gardens, with fountains, grottoes and shady bowers, were laid out in the 15th century.

Places to Eat

① **Trattoria La Fiasca, Sirmione**

MAP G4 ■ Via Santa Maria Maggiore 11 ■ 030-990-6111 ■ Closed Wed, Jan– early Feb ■ €€

This local favourite has an inviting atmosphere and a menu featuring dishes such as gnocchi with speck, mushrooms and local Baqòs cheese.

② **Antica Hostaria Cavallino, Desenzano**

MAP G4 ■ Via Gherla 30 ■ 030-912-0217 ■ Closed Mon & Nov ■ €€€

This restaurant offers local dishes and freshly caught lake fish, along with an exceptional wine list.

③ **Villa Fiordaliso, Gardone Riviera**

MAP G4 ■ Via Zanardelli 150 ■ 0365-20-158 ■ Closed Mon & Nov–Feb ■ €€€

A gorgeous Art Nouveau villa-hotel, serving local, seasonal produce in dazzling modern dishes (see p66).

④ **La Rucola, Sirmione**

MAP G4 ■ Via Strentelle 3 ■ 030-916-326 ■ Closed Jan–mid-Feb ■ €€€

The Bignotti family's genteel restaurant offers a creative menu based on seasonal ingredients and local fish and meats.

⑤ **Gemma, Limone**

MAP G3 ■ Piazza Garibaldi 12 ■ 0365-954-014 ■ €€

A charming, family-run place with a waterside terrace. Lake fish and organic meats feature on the menu.

⑥ **Tenuta Canova, Lazise**

MAP G4 ■ Via Delaini 1 ■ 045-758-0239 ■ Closed Sun eve, Jan–mid-Feb, Sep–Dec: Tue ■ €€

Part of the prestigious Masi wine-making group, this vineyard hostelry puts the emphasis on the wine, with suggested pairings for each dish on the menu, which includes guinea-fowl and gnocchi with smoked ricotta.

⑦ **Vecchia Malcesine, Malcesine**

MAP H3 ■ Via Pisort 6 ■ 045-740-0469 ■ Closed Wed & Nov–Feb ■ €€€

Enjoy lake specialities and lake views on the panoramic terrace here.

Interior of the Vecchia Malcesine

⑧ **Osteria dell'Orologio, Salò**

MAP G4 ■ Via Butturini 26 ■ 03-6529-0158 ■ Closed Wed & 3 wks Jan ■ €

This historic hostelry serves dishes such as pasta with Bagòs cheese or duck, and grilled lake fish with polenta, plus excellent local wines.

⑨ **Trattoria da Pino Due, Garda**

MAP G4 ■ Via dell'Uva 17 ■ 045-725-5694 ■ Closed Mon & Jan–Feb ■ €

A popular trattoria just outside Garda itself, with a wide shady veranda, serving delicious home cooking.

⑩ **Ristorante Gardesana, Torri del Benaco**

MAP G4 ■ Piazza Calderini 5 ■ 045-722-5411 ■ Closed Mon & Nov–Mar ■ €€€

Book ahead for a table on the long terrace overlooking the harbour. Great local and international food.

See map on p120 ←

☷ Smaller Lakes and Towns

While it is true that the lakes of Maggiore, Como and Garda are the best-developed and most obvious tourist destinations of the region, do not overlook the lesser-known lakes and towns of Lombardy. The museums of Bergamo, Mantua and others may not be as important as Milan's, the villas less grand than Como's, but a few days spent off the beaten path can offer a rewarding break from the crowds that throng Milan's great sights and back up traffic for hours along the big three lakes.

Harbourside, Lake Mergozza

1 Lake Mergozzo

MAP A2 ■ Granite Museum: Via Roma 4; 0323-670-731; open Jul & Aug: 3–6pm Tue–Sun; Sep, Oct, Mar–Jun: 3–6pm Sat & Sun; www.ecomuseo granitomontorfano.it

Once part of Lake Maggiore and still joined by a 3-km (2-mile) canal, Lake Mergozzo has clear water, idyllic for swimming, while the lack of strong winds makes it a favourite among kayakers. Mergozzo town itself is a delightful place with cobbled lanes colourful buildings and an ancient elm tree which has stood in the main piazza for at least 400 years. The area is famous for its granite, and there's a museum here dedicated to the local quarrying tradition and history.

SMALLER LAKES AND TOWNS

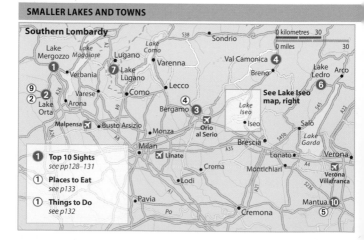

Southern Lombardy

- ❶ **Top 10 Sights** see pp128–131
- ① **Places to Eat** see p133
- ① **Things to Do** see p132

Sacro Monte di San Francesco, above Lake Orta

2 Lake Orta
MAP A3 ■ Tourist info: Via Panoramica in Orta S Giulio; 0322-905-163; www.lagodorta.piemonte.it ■ Sacro Monte: www.sacrimonti.net

Just west of Lake Maggiore, this delightful little lake amid mountains and woodlands has a smattering of picturesque fishing villages around its shores. The star of the show is the exquisite medieval village of Orta San Giulio and its Piazza Motta. Nearby, Sacro Monte is a series of 20 chapels with statues portraying the life of St Franci. Just offshore is Isola San Giulio, dominated by the Romanesque basilica of San Giulio which has some remarkable frescoes, the earliest from the 14th century.

3 Bergamo
A beguiling, vibrant city of medieval streets, fashionable boutiques and Renaissance churches, Bergamo is a favourite with Italians and tourists. A cable-car links its upper medieval and lower modern town (see pp32–3).

4 Val Camonica
MAP F2 ■ Tourist info: Via S Briscioli 42, Capo di Ponte; 0364-42-080; www.invallecamonica.it

The villages of Capo di Ponte and Nadro di Ceto are the best access points for a visit to see one of the largest groupings of prehistoric rock carvings in the world. It is thought there are 200–300,000 images to be found in this valley north of Lake Iseo. The earliest images are at least 3,000 years old and include hunting scenes with deer and elk.

Val Camonica rock carvings

Fraciacorta vineyards and winery

5 Franciacorta
MAP D3 ■ Franciacorta Tourist Board: www.franciacorta.net

A wine-making area since ancient Roman times, the Franciacorta hills are home to some of Italy's best sparkling wines. Many wineries offer tours and tastings (see p132). Other attractions include the San Pietro monastery, overlooking the Torbiere nature reserve, and Castello Quistini with its fabulous rose garden.

6 Lake Ledro
MAP D3 ■ www.valledilledro. com ■ Museo delle Palafitte: www. palafitteledro.it

This idyllic lake in the mountains just west of Riva del Garda is a relaxing alternative to its larger neighbour.

The pretty ferry port of Pescheria on Monte Isola, viewed from Lake Iseo

There are four beaches, and canoing, walking and mountain-biking are available. The incredible discovery of over 10,000 pillars from Bronze Age stilt-houses was made in the early 20th century; a fascinating recon-struction of such a village sits on the lakeside at the Museo delle Palafitte museum in Molina.

7 Lake Lugano
MAP B2–C2 ■ Tourist info: Campione d'Italia; Via Volta 3; www. campioneitalia.com ■ Swiss Miniatur: adm; www.swissminiatur.ch

Lake Lugano's principal resort, Campione d'Italia, is an Italian enclave within Switzerland's borders. To the south, outside Melide, is the delightfully kitsch Swiss Miniatur, whose "map" of Switzerland, covers all of the country's major monu-ments at 1/25 of their actual size.

8 Monte Isola
MAP E3 ■ Bicycle hire: Mar–Sep; www.monteisolabici.it

This peaceful, traffic-free island at the centre of Lake Iseo is ideal for a day out. Bicycles can be hired at Peschiera Maraglio, and walks include the path to the Madonna della Ceriola sanctuary at the top of the island, for stunning views over the lake and surrounding mountains. Peschiera is the main ferry stop and Siviano is Monte Isola's charming little capital, while Carzanoa, on the other side of the island, is a pictur-esque fishing village.

9 Lake Iseo

MAP E3–4 ■ Tourist info: IAT Lungolago Marconi 2, Iseo; 030-374-8733; www.iseolake.info

This is the prettiest of the smaller lakes, and the town of Iseo itself is as touristy as it gets. At Lovere, Galleria Tadini has a small collection of paintings by Bellini, Tintoretto and Tiepolo. The interior of the church of Santa Maria della Neve, at Pisogne, is another delight.

Fresco, Santa Maria della Neve

10 Mantua

The palaces, churches and artworks by Mantegna and Giulio Romano help make the town of Mantua a must-visit (see pp34–5).

TWO DAYS EXPLORING LAKE ISEO AND FRANCIACORTA

▶ DAY ONE

Take an early ferry to Peschiera Maraglio on **Monte Isola** and hire a bike from the Bertelli news-agent's near the ferry stop. Cycle along the waterfront with the lake on your left to reach Siviano. Explore the village and continue to Carzano, stopping for a swim to work up an appetite for a lunch of delicious lake fish specialities at **Locanda al Lago** (see p133).

Back on the mainland, head north to **Pisogne** (see p132); climb the tower and see the frescoes in the Santa Maria della Neve church. Return to Iseo in time to explore the centre and stop for a drink in Piazza Garibaldi before dinner at **Trattoria al Porto** (see p133) in Clusane, about 5 miles; stay the night at their sister B&B, **La Casa di Gabri** nearby (see p148).

DAY TWO

Have a leisurely breakfast by the pool then set off to explore the **Franciacorta** wine area. Before hitting the wineries visit the **San Pietro in Lamosa** monastery and walk the trails of the **Torbiere Nature Reserve**. If it's a Sunday in May or June, pop in to see the roses at Castello Quistini then stop for lunch at the **Solive Agriturismo** (see p133), enjoyed with a bottle of their Curtefranca.

Meet your guide from the **Franciacorta Bike Tour** (see p132) and cycle through the vines, stopping for tastings at wineries along the way. Alternatively join a prebooked tour at **Ca' del Bosco** (see p132). Stay in Erbusco for the evening with a tasty meal at **La Smorfia** trattoria (see p133).

See map on pp128–9 ←

Things to Do

 Wine-Tasting in Franciacorta

MAP D3 ▪ Ca' de Bosco: www.cadelbosco.com

Most of the wineries offer tours and tastings. The prestigious Ca' del Bosco winery combines art and wine; even the entrance gate is a sculpture.

2 Lovere

MAP D3 ▪ Accademia Tadini: Via Tadini 40; 035-962-2780; Adm; www.accademiatadini.it

Lovere features a waterfront piazza and an intriguing maze of lanes. The Accademia Tadini has a fine collection, with works by Canova and Bellini.

3 Pisogne

MAP F3

The 13th-century Torre del Vescovo tower dominates this pretty Lake Iseo village. Santa Maria della Neve has Renaissance frescoes *(see p131)*.

 Cycle Routes

Franciacorta Bike Tour: www.franciacortabiketour.com ▪ Iseo Bike: www.iseobike.com

A bicycle is the perfect vehicle for exploring the Franciacorta wine area. The Vello–Tolino path is popular.

Cycling in Franciacorta

5 Golf

MAP D3 ▪ Franciacorta Golf Club: Via Provinciale 34B, Corte Franca; www.franciacortagolfclub.it

The Franciacorta golf club has an immaculate 36-hole course. For non-golfers there's a wellness area, swimming pool and tennis courts.

6 Treno dei Sapori

MAP E4 ▪ trenodeisapori.area3v.com

Book for a gourmet experience with a difference on this historic train. The trips depart from Iseo and include guided tours, tastings and meals of local foods and wines. On some routes you can make your return by boat.

7 Antica Strada Valeriana

MAP F3 ▪ Lake Iseo: www.iseolake.info

The ancient cobbled Antica Valeriana is a simple footpath with idyllic views linking Pisogne with Pilzone, passing the glacial erosion pyramids at Zone.

8 Watersports

Experience Lake Iseo from the water, either by kayak, windsurfer, kitesurfer or SUP. Tuition and hire is available at various points around the lake including Iseo and Marone.

9 Lake Iseo Cruises

MAP E4 ▪ www.navigazionelagoiseo.it

Cruises touring the islands of Monte Isola, San Paolo and Loreto offer a memorable viewpoint over the lake and surrounding mountains.

10 Torbiere Nature Reserve

MAP G3 ▪ Visitor Centre: Via Tangenziale Sud, Iseo; www.torbieresebino.it

This evocative expanse of lakes and marshland was once a peat bog, There's now a network of nature trails and a well-placed observation tower. Binoculars can be borrowed for free from the Visitor Centre to spot the diverse range of wildlife here.

Places to Eat

1 Trattoria al Porto, Lake Iseo

MAP E4 ▪ Piazza Porto dei Pescatori 12, Clusane sul Lago ▪ 030-989 014 ▪ Closed Wed ▪ €€

Spaghetti with lake prawns and ravioli with Bagòs cheese are among the high-lights at this rustic-chic trattoria run by the Bosio family since 1862 *(see p66)*.

Villa Crespi's exotic dining room

2 Villa Crespi, Lake Orta

MAP A3 ▪ Via G Fava 18, San Giulio ▪ 0322-911-902 ▪ Closed Mon & lunch Tue; Nov & Dec: Tue eve; Jan–Mar ▪ €€€

This stylish restaurant, in a unique Moorish-fantasy hotel *(see p148)*, promises elegant service and top-quality regional cuisine.

3 Trattoria Bali, Lake Iseo

MAP D3 ▪ Via IV Novembre 4, Lovere ▪ 035-960-572 ▪ Closed Sun & mid-Aug–early Sep ▪ €

A welcoming trattoria just outside Lovere. Try the casoncelli pasta with bacon and sage, handmade by Ferdinanda for over 30 years.

4 Taverna del Colleoni dell'Angelo, Bergamo

MAP D3 ▪ Piazza Vecchia 7, Bergamo ▪ 035-232-596 ▪ Closed Mon & first week of Jan ▪ €€€

Formal restaurant in an evocative Renaissance palazzo on the main piazza, with outdoor dining in the summer. They serve local specialities.

5 Ochina Bianca, Mantua

MAP H6 ▪ Via Finzi 2 ▪ 0376-323-700 ▪ Closed Mon, Sun eve ▪ €€€

Distinctive variations on local dishes and a judicious use of fresh fish from the nearby Mincio River.

6 La Smorfia, Erbusco

MAP D3 ▪ Via Costa 9 ▪ 030-726-8434 ▪ Closed Tue ▪ €

Pizzas, gourmet burgers, traditional dishes and a monthly spit roast. Being Franciacorta, the wine list is superb: ask owner Enrico for advice.

7 Solive Agriturismo, Nigoline di Corte Franca

MAP D3 ▪ Via Calvarole 15 ▪ 030-988-4201 ▪ Closed Mon eve, Tue ▪ €€

Try this farm's own grilled meats together with a bottle of their full-bodied red Curtefranca.

8 VistaLago Bistrò, Erbusco

MAP D3 ▪ Via Vittorio Emanuele 23 ▪ 030-776-0550 ▪ €€€

Come to L'Albereta hotel *(see p148)* for a hot and cold Sunday brunch and fabulous views over Lake Iseo.

9 Al Boeuc, Lake Orta

MAP A3 ▪ Via Bersani 28, Orta San Giulio ▪ 339-584-0039 ▪ Closed Mar–Oct: Tue; winter, if no booking ▪ €

Good wine, regional dishes such as *bagna cauda*, and platters of local meats and cheeses are served here.

10 Locanda al Lago, Lake Iseo

MAP E3 ▪ Località Carzano 38 ▪ 030-988-6472 ▪ Closed Tue (except May–mid-Sep) ▪ €€

Run by a local fishing family, this is the place to enjoy fish-stuffed ravioli or the island's own smoked salami.

See map on pp128–9

Streetsmart

Old and new side-by-side in Milan's booming Porta Nuova district

Getting To and Around Milan and the Lakes

Arriving by Air

Milan has two primary airports: **Milan Malpensa**, the main hub, has intercontinental flights plus domestic and European connections. The airport's two terminals are linked by a free 24-hour shuttle; travel time between them is 15 minutes. Malpensa is about 40 km (25 miles) northwest of the city. The railway station is located at Terminal 1 and Terminal 2 and Milan Express trains run every 30 minutes to Milan Cadorna station, near Castello Sforzesco, and less frequently to Milan Central station. Various bus services connect Malpensa with the city's central station, including **Autostradale**, **Terravision**, and **Malpensa Express**. **Alibus** runs a shuttle bus between the airport and Lake Maggiore from March to October.

Milan Linate, just 7 km (4 miles) from the city centre, is Milan's second airport. The number 73 **ATM** city bus runs every 10 minutes between the airport and Piazza San Babila in central Milan, taking about 30 minutes. Autostradale runs shuttle services to the city centre, and the **Malpensa Shuttle** runs a shuttle between the city's two airports.

Bergamo's **Orio al Serio** airport is roughly 50 km (30 miles) east of Milan and connected to the city by Terravision, **Orio Shuttle** and Autostradale buses. Orio Shuttle and **ATB** also run bus services into Bergamo; the journey takes about 15 minutes. Milan's airports are the nearest for Lake Maggiore and Lake Como, but **Verona** airport is more convenient for Lake Garda. **ATV** runs buses to Lake Garda that take about an hour.

Arriving by Road

There are road tunnels through the Alps linking Italy to Switzerland and France, as well as coast roads from France and Slovenia. Northern Italy has an efficient network of motorways and the **Autostrade per l'Italia** website has live traffic updates. Tolls are paid on leaving the motorway; it can be quicker to pay by credit card at one of the dedicated booths (no commission is charged).

Eurolines and **Flixbus** both operate budget long-distance bus services linking cities throughout Europe and Italy, including Milan, Verona, Mantua, Bergamo and Como.

Arriving and Getting Around by Train

Trenitalia and **Italo** trains run between major cities, with good links throughout Europe. The local rail network is run by Trenitalia, and **Trenord** for Lombardy.

The journey time from Milan to Stresa on Lake Maggiore is around an hour; to Como it is just over 30 minutes. Trains to Desenzano on Lake Garda take 50 minutes from Milan or 20 minutes from Verona, and to reach Iseo you will need to change at Brescia. The journey time from Milan to Verona is just over an hour; from Milan to Mantua it is an hour and 50 minutes.

Tickets for all but the high-speed trains should be stamped at machines near the platform to be validated before boarding.

Getting Around by Car

Driving in Milan can be a nightmare, with limited traffic zones (ZTL), tram- or bus-only lanes and pedestrianized areas, but a car is the best way to explore more remote parts of the region. Around the lakes, roads get extremely busy in summer and parking is scarce; here ferries are often the best option.

Parking spaces marked in blue require payment, yellow-lined spaces are reserved for residents and white spaces mean you can park for free, unless otherwise shown.

Getting Around by Bus, Tram or Metro

ATM operates the buses, trams and metro in Milan. The same ticket is valid for all three and should be bought in advance at newsagents, tobacconists and some bars. Stamp the ticket in the machine by the bus or tram doors to validate it when you get on. Tickets can also be bought though the ATM Milano mobile app (an

English version is available]. These are validated via the app on your device when you board the bus or tram.

Individual tickets (€1.50) are valid for 90 minutes and you can change freely between buses and trams within this time, but may only include one journey by Metro or on Trenord trains within the urban area. Day passes, which cost €4.50, and two-day passes (€8.25) are valid for unlimited journeys on all local services.

Milan has four metro lines. Ticket information for the Metro is the same as for buses and trams, but tickets bought via the app must be scanned each time you pass through the turnstiles.

There is a useful online journey planner, called **Muoversi in Lombardia**.

Getting Around by Bicycle

Cycle lanes in Milan are on the increase and the city runs a bike-sharing scheme with numerous access points. Both daily (€4.50) and weekly (€9) subscriptions are available, but each journey must have a maximum duration of 2 hours. Subscribe via the **BikeMi** website or mobile app, by calling the info-line or at an ATM info-point.

Smile and Bike rents bicycles at points around the city and runs bicyle tours. Bike hire is widely available at the lakes.

Getting Around on Foot

Central Milan is relatively compact and there are many pedestrianized areas in the centre. At the lakes, towns and villages often have steep, narrow lanes with cobblestones or steps, tricky for people with reduced mobility.

Getting Around the Lakes by Ferry

Travelling by ferry is the best way to get around the lakes. **Gestione Navigazione Laghi** runs regular ferry services on Lakes Maggiore, Como and Garda, including both car and passenger-only ferries, while **Navigazione Lago Iseo** is the operator for Lake Iseo. Both also offer specialist cruises.

Single-journey and all-day tickets are available. Each jetty has its own ticket office which, in quieter periods, opens only about 20 minutes before a ferry is due.

DIRECTORY

ARRIVING BY AIR

Alibus
w safduemila.com

ATB
w atb.bergamo.it

ATM
w atm.it

ATV
w atv.verona.it

Autostradale
w airportbusexpress.it

Malpensa Express
w malpensaexpress.it

Malpensa Shuttle
w malpensashuttle.it

Milan Linate Airport
w milanolinate-airport.com

Milan Malpensa Airport
w milanomalpensa-airport.com

Orio al Serio Airport
w orioaeroporto.it

Orio Shuttle
w orioshuttle.com

Terravision
w terravision.eu

Verona Airport
w aeroportoverona.it

ARRIVING BY ROAD

Autostrade per l'Italia
w autostrade.it
C 840 042121

Eurolines
w eurolines.com

Flixbus
w flixbus.com

ARRIVING AND GETTING AROUND BY TRAIN

Italo
w italotreno.it

Trenitalia
w trenitalia.com

Trenord
w trenord.it

GETTING AROUND BY BUS, TRAM OR METRO

Muoversi in Lombardia
w muoversi.regione.lombardia.it

GETTING AROUND BY BICYCLE

BikeMi
w bikemi.com;
C 02-4860-7607

Smile and Bike
w smileandbike.com

GETTING AROUND THE LAKES BY FERRY

Gestione Navigazione Laghi (Lakes Maggiore, Como and Garda)
C 031 579211
w navlaghi.it

Navigazione Lago Iseo
C 035 971483
w navigazionelagoiseo.it

Practical Information

Passports and Visas

Visas are not required for visitors to Italy from other countries within the European Union (EU), the European Economic Area (EEA) or Switzerland, but a valid identity card or passport is necessary. People travelling from a number of non-European countries such as Canada, the US, Brazil, Australia, New Zealand and Japan can stay for up to 90 days without a visa. For further information on visa regulations consult the **Ministero degli Esteri**.

Customs and Immigration

There are no limits in place on most goods carried between EU countries, including alcohol and tobacco, as long as they are just for personal use. Restrictions apply to firearms and other weapons, animals and some types of food. Arrivals from outside the EU can bring 16 litres of beer and 4 litres of wine, along with 1 litre of spirits or 2 litres of fortified wine; 250g (8.8 oz) of tobacco; and other dutiable goods of up to €430 in value. Amounts of cash over €10,000 taken into or out of the EU must be declared. Non-EU citizens can apply for VAT refunds on goods bought in the EU.

Travel Safety Advice

Visitors can get up-to-date travel safety information from the **UK Foreign and Commonwealth Office**, the **US Department of State** as well as the **Australian Department of Foreign Affairs and Trade**.

Travel Insurance

As with any trip, it is advisable to take out travel insurance to cover healthcare emergencies, transport cancellations, theft and loss. EU citizens carrying an **EHIC** European Health Insurance Card are entitled to free emergency healthcare thanks to a reciprocal arrangement with other EU countries, but prescriptions and non-emergency healthcare must be paid for and can be costly. Australian citizens can also benefit from the **RHCA** Reciprocal Health Care Agreement when in Italy.

Health

No vaccinations are required for visiting Italy and there are no particular health hazards in and around Milan and the lakes. Emergency treatment is provided free of charge at hospitals with a casualty department (pronto soccorso) but there is often a long wait unless it's a serious emergency. Hospitals with casualty departments in Milan include **Ospedale Fatebenefratelli**, **Ospedale Maggiore Policlinico**, and **Ospedale Macedonio Melloni**. On the lakes there are **Ospedale Castelli** (Lake Maggiore), **Ospedale Valduce** (Lake Como), **Ospedale di Lovere** (Lake Iseo) and **Ospedale di Desenzano** (Lake Garda). The **International Health Center** in central Milan has a weekdays-only team of English-speaking doctors and dentists and appointments are usually available at short notice. Free and anonymous testing for sexually transmitted diseases (STDs) is available at the walk-in **CRH-MTS** clinic.

Pharmacies have a green cross sign outside and are the best place to go for minor ailments, as they give well-informed advice and sell over-the-counter medication. When closed they always display the name and address of the nearest out-of-hours pharmacy. The **Boccaccio Pharmacy**, near the Santa Maria delle Grazie church which houses Leonardo Da Vinci's *Last Supper*, is open 24 hours a day, seven days a week.

Personal Security

Milan is a relatively safe city and doesn't present any particular threats to personal security, although the usual sensible precautions should, of course, be taken with money, credit cards and valuables, especially in crowded areas and on public transport. Don't leave items of value visible in a parked car. Women travelling alone should not encounter particular problems in Milan or around the lakes. For most emergencies it's advisable to call the general **emergency**

number, but there are also numbers for the state police, the fire service and ambulances.

The **Polizia di Stato** (state police) and the **Carabinieri** (military police) have similar roles, and thefts should be reported to one or the other. There are a number of police stations and Carabinieri stations in Milan and on the lakes. A stolen credit and debit cards should be blocked immediately by calling the 24-hour Polizia di Stato number. The **Polizia Ferroviaria** (railway police) are present at main stations and can be asked about items lost on trains.

Report lost items to the city's **Oggetti Smarriti** (lost property) office.

Currency and Banking

Italy's currency is the euro (€). Euro notes come in denominations of 500, 200, 100, 50, 20, 10 and 5 euros, while the coin denominations are 2 and 1 euros, then 50, 20, 10, 5, 2 and 1 cents. The easiest way to get cash is to use a debit or credit card at an ATM (bancomat), and these are easily found in central and suburban Milan. ATMs are also common in all but the smallest villages around

the lakes. Commission for exchanging cash is lower at post offices than at banks, while bureaux de change generally have the least favourable rates. Credit cards are becoming more widely accepted in Italy, especially Visa and MasterCard, however some small restaurants will only take cash so check before ordering.

Electrical Appliances

Italy's power supply is 230 volts. Italian plugs have two or three round pins and devices from most other countries will need to have an adaptor.

DIRECTORY

PASSPORTS & VISAS

Ministero degli Esteri
w vistoperitalia.esteri.it/home/en

TRAVEL SAFETY ADVICE

Australian Department of Foreign Affairs and Trade
w dfat.gov.au
w smarttraveller.gov.au

UK Foreign and Commonwealth Office
w gov.uk/foreign-travel-advice

US Department of State
w travel.state.gov

TRAVEL INSURANCE

EHIC
w gov.uk/european-health-insurance-cardl

RHCA
w humanservices.gov.au

HEALTH

Boccaccio Pharmacy
Via Boccaccio 26, Milan

CRH-MTS
Viale Jenner 44, Milan
(02 8578 9871

International Health Center
Galleria Strasburgo 3, San Babila, Milan
(02 7634 0720;
w ihc.it

Ospedale Castelli
Via Fiume 18, Verbania

Ospedale di Desenzano
Località Montecroce, Desenzano

Ospedale Fatebenefratelli
Corso di Porta Nuova 23

Ospedale di Lovere
Via Martinoli 9, Lovere

Ospedale Macedonio Melloni
Via Macedonio Melloni 52, Milan

Ospedale Maggiore Policlinico
Via San Barnaba 8, Milan

Ospedale Valduce
Via Santo Garovaglio 14, Como

PERSONAL SECURITY

Ambulances
(118

Carabinieri
Via Fosse Ardeatine 4, Milan
Via Dalla Chiesa 1, Verbania
Piazzale Duca d'Aosta 1, Como
Via Marconi 57, Desenzano del Garda

Emergency number
(112

Fire Service
(115

Oggetti Smarriti
Via Friuli 30, Milan
(02 8845 3900

Polizia Ferroviaria
Stazione Centrale, Milan
(02 6692106

Polizia di Stato
(113
Piazza San Sepolcro 9, Milan
Piazza Venino 6, Milan
Via Fatebenefratelli 11, Milan
Corso Nazioni Unite 18, Pallanza
Via Roosevelt 7, Como
Via Roma 102, Iseo
Via Dante Alighieri 17, Desenzano del Garda

Telephone and Internet

If you are an EU resident, roaming charges for using your mobile phone within Europe were abolished as of 15 June 2017, so costs are now the same as for using it at home. Visitors from other nations will find it cheaper to invest in a pay-as-you-go Italian sim card; Tim, Vodafone, Wind and Tre are the main providers. Payphones are becoming increasingly difficult to find but can be used with a prepaid phone card *(scheda telefonica)* which can be bought at newsagents.

Area dialling codes (beginning with 0) must be dialled within Italy even for local calls; Italian mobile phone numbers begin with 3. International country codes should be preceded by 00 (for the UK 44, for Australia 61) followed by the local area code minus the initial zero, and the number. For the USA and Canada you dial 001 followed by the full number.

Free Wi-Fi is widely available in Milan via the **Open WIFI Milano** service; the website has a map of the hotspots. Hotels, cafés and bars also often provide free Wi-Fi, and so do both Milan Malpensa and Milan Linate airports as well as the Autogrill motorway service stations, and it's usually available on high-speed trains.

Postal Services

The flat rate for sending letters and cards within Europe is €1, and €2.20 to North America. Stamps *(francobolli)* are sold at tobacconists *(tabacchi)* which are recognisable by a large blue or black letter "T" sign; queuing at post offices can be a frustrating experience as service is often very slow. Postboxes are red and can often be found outside tobacconists as well as at post offices. Pre-franked postcards, linked to private postal services, are sometimes available in tourist hot spots, but they should be avoided as they tend to cost more and take longer to be delivered.

TV, Radio and Newspapers

Most hotels in Italy now have satellite TV with international channels. **IsoRadio** is a national radio station (103.3 FM and online) which offers frequent updates on traffic problems, with bulletins in English during the summer. International newspapers and magazines are available at newsagents throughout Milan and, during the high season, in the larger resorts around the lakes.

Opening Hours

In central Milan the majority of shops open at about 9am and close around 7:30–8pm seven days a week. Smaller shops, neighbourhood food stores and banks traditionally open around 8am and close between 12:30–1pm and 3:30–4pm, then stay open until about 7.30pm (though banks close earlier) and are closed on Sundays.

Non-stop opening hours *(orario continuato)* are becoming more widespread, however, and opening times should be displayed. Churches observe similar hours to shops, while most museums remain open all day from Tuesday to Sunday but are closed on Mondays and last entry is usually 30 minutes before the official closing time.

Time Difference

Italy operates on Central European Time (CET), which is 1 hour ahead of Greenwich Mean Time and 6 hours ahead of US Eastern Standard Time. The clock moves forward by 1 hour during daylight saving time from the last Sunday in March until the last Sunday in October.

Weather

Milan has a climate of extremes: very hot and humid in summer (many shops and restaurants close down for much of August) and cold in winter, so late spring and early autumn are the most pleasant times to visit.

The lakes benefit from a much milder microclimate, as can be seen from the luxuriant and often exotic vegetation, but many of the villas and gardens are closed during winter, as are a lot of hotels and restaurants. During May, June and September the famous gardens are looking their very best and these are, once again, the best times for a visit, particularly since the whole lakes area can get extremely busy in July and August.

Disabled Travellers

The excellent **Milano Per Tutti** website has extensive listings of museums, galleries, churches, restaurants and hotels with exhaustive details of accessibility, aimed at people with all kinds of disabilities, and there's also a series of suggested itineraries for visitors to the city as well as advice on transport.

Italian airports and railway stations have very well-organized assistance for disabled travellers. Most of the larger, more modern hotels have wheelchair facilities, but bars and restaurants are sometimes lacking. There may be problems due to the age and architecture of the particular building.

At the lakes, the hillside villages can be hard to navigate due to the steep, narrow lanes, cobbles and flights of steps.

Many upmarket hotels now offer gluten-free breakfast options and restaurants occasionally have dedicated menus. Staff are usually sensitive to special dietary requirements regarding allergies.

Sources of Information

The biggest and busiest office of **Turismo Milano**, the city's tourist department, is in the Galleria Vittorio Emanuele II, on the corner of Piazza della Scala. **Where Milan** is a free magazine and website with a wealth of information on places to stay and things to do, as well as restaurants, clubs, sights, shops and events. The **Lake Como Tourist** Office, the **Lake Iseo & Franciacorta Tourist Office,** the **Lake Garda Tourist Office,** and the **Lake Maggiore & Orta Tourist office** can provide information on events, tours, hotels, restaurants, sights and sports facilities.

Trips and Tours

Milano City Sightseeing runs hop-on-hop-off tours around the city by double-decker bus; the price of the ticket includes headphones and there's a registered commentary in a number of languages. Guided walking tours (in English or Italian) of the Historic Centre of Milan are run by **Milan Free Tour**, and are completely free of charge. The local transport company, ATM *(see p137)* has converted two historic trams into attractive mobile restaurants, called **ATMosfera**, and offer tours of the city with dinner on board every night of the week. Boat trips on Milan's Navigli canals are provided by **Navigli Lombardi** and various itineraries, both long and short, are available.

Many companies offer boat tours of the lakes, and the standard ferry companies also organize various lake cruises. The Gestione Navigazione Laghi ferry services *(see p137)* cover the lakes of Maggiore, Como and Garda while Lake Iseo is covered by Navigazione Lago Iseo *(see p137)*.

A memorable way to see Lake Como is from the air with a seaplane tour; these are organized by the **Aero Club Como**.

DIRECTORY

TELEPHONE AND INTERNET

Open WIFI Milano
🅦 openwifimilano.it

TV, RADIO, AND NEWSPAPERS

IsoRadio
🅦 isoradio.rai.it

DISABLED TRAVELLERS

Milano Per Tutti
🅦 milanopertutti.it

SOURCES OF INFORMATION

Lake Como Tourist Office
🅦 lakecomo.it

Lake Garda Tourist Office
🅦 visitgarda.com
🅦 gardalombardia.com

Lake Iseo & Franciacorta Tourist Office
🅦 iseolake.info

Lake Maggiore & Lake Orta Tourist Office
🅦 distrettolaghi.it
🅦 illagomaggiore.com

Turismo Milano
🅦 turismo.milano.it

Where Milan
🅦 wheremilan.com

TRIPS AND TOURS

Aero Club Como
🅦 aeroclubcomo.com

ATMosfera
🅦 atm.it

Milano City Sightseeing
🅦 milano.city-sightseeing.it

Milan Free Tour
🅦 milanfreetour.com

Navigli Lombardi
🅦 naviglilombardi.it

Shopping

Milan is unquestionably Italy's capital of shopping. From the ultra exclusive designer boutiques of the Golden Quad to the independent offbeat stores of Corso di Porta Ticinese, there's something here for everyone. Personal shoppers exist to help those with serious spending in mind to find their way around, and **Exclusive Fashion Tours** runs a good service.

Although fashion is the main focus of the city's retail therapy opportunities, there's much more to Milan than just couture. The city has an excellent range of quality food stores, for example, and delicatessens will usually be able to vacuum pack items on request. The monthly antiques market at Navigli *(see pp28–9)* is exceptional, while football fans can score souvenirs and official strip of the city's two top teams, AC Milan and Internazionale, at **(AC) Milano Megastore** and **Inter Store Milano** located in the city centre.

The weekly open-air markets in the villages around the lakes are colourful and popular, and generally sell everything from food to clothing.

Como is well-known for its long silk tradition, and there are a number of stores selling silk items in Como and Bellagio.

Non-EU residents can claim VAT refunds on goods costing a combined total of at least €155 bought from the same store on the same day, by filling in the appropriate forms and having them stamped at customs.

Where to Eat

Milan has a vast and varied choice of eateries of every kind and for every budget. As well as Italian food, there are numerous places serving international cuisine, particularly oriental, and there's a good choice of vegetarian eateries around the city.

Although nowadays the lines dividing the different categories of restaurant have become blurred, a *ristorante* traditionally offers a more formal dining experience, while a trattoria serves simple home cooking and is often family run. An *osteria* originally referred to a wine bar with food, whereas nowadays the term is used for a low-key eatery with a relaxed atmosphere – they are now more frequently called *enoteca con cucina*. Pizzerias are abundant, and usually serve a simple restaurant menu as well as pizzas, which are sometimes available in the evenings only.

Eateries of all kinds tend to open from about noon to 2:30 or 3pm and from about 7 to 10pm, or later in busy areas. Food is served all day in some places at busy holiday times around the lakes.

Cafés often have ready-prepared hot *(tavola calda)* or cold *(tavola fredda)* food and they are increasingly providing freshly cooked dishes too. Brunch is often served at weekends, and most bars and cafés provide a generous buffet of snacks from about 6pm to 8 or 9pm each evening; there's often a set price for drinks at this time, to include the food, which is sometimes substantial and may even include pasta or other hot dishes. Enticing delicatessens *(gastronomia)* are the best choice for *panini* (sandwiches), made with top quality ingredients, while markets and food shops are the place to go for putting a picnic together.

Menus are divided into *antipasti* (starters), *primi* (pasta or rice), *secondi* (a main course of fish or meat, sometimes with vegetarian options), *contorni* (side dishes), *formaggi* (cheeses) and *dolci* (dessert). Although a traditional Italian meal would include at least three of these, it's quite acceptable to order just one or two courses from any section of the menu. Side dishes will be served with the main course but the other courses will be served in sequence, unless you specify that you want them at the same time (*insieme* means together).

Most menus offer a house wine and a choice of wine by the bottle, if not a full, and often extensive, wine list. Tap water, even though it's drinkable, is rarely served, but still *(naturale)* or sparkling *(frizzante)* mineral water will always be offered.

Larger eateries often have high-chairs for small children and sometimes there is a special menu; if not, most places will happily serve half portions *(mezza porzione)* or simple dishes, such as pasta with tomato sauce *(pasta al pomodoro)* even if these are not on the menu.

Italians rarely leave tips unless the service has been truly exceptional. Watch out for extra service charges added as a percentage, particularly in the tourist resorts.

Where to Stay

There's a good choice of hotels at all levels in Milan itself and near the lakes, where there is an exceptional selection of quality hotels located in historic lakeside villas. Direct booking is favoured by many of the smaller hotels but international booking websites such as **Booking.com**, have an excellent range of options. The number of B&Bs in Italy is growing rapidly, and this relatively recent accommodation option often provides the best deals in terms of comfort, style, price and location and hosts are often keen to help with local advice. **Bed & Breakfast Italia** is a well-arranged website with a wide range of properties, and their BBcard offers a loyalty discount to members. **Homestay** also has a small selection of hosts offering – mostly simple and inexpensive but stylish – private rooms in Milan.

Self-catering offers both flexibility and the chance to shop for and cook local produce. Online booking organizations such as **Home Away** and **Airbnb** have plenty of options in and around Milan. There is also a good choice of self-catering options at the lakes. As well as the online booking agencies there are some good local agencies with lovely properties of all sizes and styles – for Lake Como try **Vacanze Lago**, or **Garda Holidays** and **Lake Maggiore Homes**.

Waterside campsites are a popular option for holidays at the lakes; they often have direct access to the water and some-times offer watersports on site as well as having other sporting facilities. Accommodation is often available at working farms, called *agriturismo*, where farm experiences, inter-action with farmyard animals for children, cookery courses, wine-tasting and a host of other experiences are some-times available. Note that the term refers to farms with either a restaurant or accommodation but not necessarily both. The **Parco Agricolo Sud Milano** website lists a good range of *agriturismi* in the Milan area, with details of what they offer, while **Agriturismo Italia** is the official national website and has a full list of recognized *agriturismi*. **Agriturist** is another good website for listings, with information in English.

Hostel World lists budget accommodation in hostels, B&Bs, camp-sites and apartments.

The local tourist boards *(see p141)* can also provide information and contacts for accommodation.

Rates and Booking

Better deals can often be obtained by booking direct with a hotel rather than online and some, partic-ularly the smaller hotels, prefer to interact with clients themselves, not always even requiring a deposit for short stay.

Breakfast, parking and use of facilities such as wellness areas and bikes may not be included in the price quoted so it's wise to check before confirming. One extra cost is the *tassa di soggiorno* or tourist tax. This is a municipal tax imposed on the first four nights you stay at any type of accommodation and varies, depending on the local regulations, category and the time of year, from 50 cents to several euros a night per person.

DIRECTORY

SHOPPING

(AC) Milan Megastore
Galleria San Carlo Corso Vittorio Emanuele II

Exclusive Fashion Tours
W exclusivefashiontours.com

Inter Store Milano
Galleria Passarella 2

WHERE TO STAY

Agriturismo Italia
W agriturismoitalia.gov.it

Agriturist
W agriturist.it

Airbnb
W airbnb.com

Bed & Breakfast Italia
W bed-and-breakfast.it

Booking.com
W booking.com

Garda Holidays
W gardaholidays.co.uk

Home Away
W homeaway.it

Homestay
W homestay.com

Hostel World
W italian.hostelworld.com

Lake Maggiore Homes
W lakemaggiorehomes.net

Parco Agricolo Sud Milano
W parcoagricolosudmilano.it

Vacanze Lago
W vacanzelago.com

Places to Stay

PRICE CATEGORIES
For a double room with breakfast and taxes in high season.

€ under €150 €€ €150–250 €€€ over €250

Milan's Luxury Hotels

Antica Locanda dei Mercanti
MAP L3 ▪ Via San Tomaso 6 ▪ 02-805-4080 ▪ www.locanda.it ▪ €€€
This 18th-century former apartment building, set between the Duomo and Castello, is a wonderful home-away-from-home. The light-filled rooms offer pale furnishings and wrought-iron bedsteads plus the occasional exposed beam. The more expensive terrazzo rooms have flower-filled rooftop terraces and canopy beds. There is also a small restaurant and bar.

Armani Hotel
MAP M3 ▪ Via Manzoni 31 ▪ 02-8883-8888 ▪ milan.armanihotels.com ▪ €€€
Rooms are decorated with Armani's signature chic and sophisticated style. There's a well-equipped 24-hour gym as well as a soothing spa, and the hotel also features a stylish Michelin-starred restaurant. The hotel's location in the heart of Milan's shopping area is perfect for retail therapy.

Carlton Hotel Baglioni
MAP N2 ▪ Via Senato 5 ▪ 02-77-077 ▪ www.baglionihotels.com ▪ €€€
This hotel, located on the north side of the shopping district, has 19th-century-style silk brocades and inlaid furnishings. There is also a business centre, a spa and a restaurant.

Four Seasons
MAP N2 ▪ Via Gesù 8 ▪ 02-77-088 ▪ www.fourseasons.com/milan ▪ €€€
The Four Seasons was converted in 1993 from a 15th-century convent, and retains some fine frescoes. The superior rooms are on the street side, while deluxe rooms open onto the cloisters. Milan's best shops are nearby, and there are two restaurants, one offering a vegetarian menu.

Grand Hotel et de Milan
MAP M3 ▪ Via Manzoni 29 ▪ 02-723-141 ▪ www.grandhoteletdemilan.it ▪ €€€
The Grand has been Milan's most intimate luxury hotel since 1863, a darling of inveterate shoppers and La Scala stars (it was Callas's Milan home). Composer Giuseppe Verdi was also a resident for 30 years.

Park Hyatt Milan
MAP L3 ▪ Via Tommaso Grossi 1 ▪ 02-8821 1234 ▪ www.milan.park.hyatt.com ▪ €€€
This luxurious hotel is situated in the heart of the city, just steps from Piazza Duomo and the Scala opera house, and within easy access of Via Montenapoleone's shops. The Ed Tuttle-designed interior features Bang & Olufsen TVs, large marble bathrooms and walk-in closets. There is also a spa with a fitness centre, gold mosaic whirlpool, men's and women's steam rooms and a hammam.

Principe di Savoia
MAP N1 ▪ Piazza della Repubblica 17 ▪ 02-623-0555 ▪ www.hotelprincipedisavoia.com ▪ €€€
Built in 1927 in true Neo-Classical Lombard style, this is probably the most elegant of Milan's top hotels. Its Principe Tower was built in 2000 for business people who like to holiday with modern conveniences.

Sheraton Diana Majestic
MAP P2 ▪ Viale Piave 42 ▪ 02-20-581 ▪ www.sheratondianamajestic.com ▪ €€€
This Liberty-style hotel set around a lush court-yard garden. The rooms have a modern elegance and lovely furniture with top-end amenities such as Bose Wave stereos.

Spadari al Duomo
MAP L4 ▪ Via Spadari 11 ▪ 02-7200-2371 ▪ www.spadarihotel.com ▪ €€€
This gem of a hotel, filled with original works by contemporary artists, is situated near Piazza Duomo. Stylish rooms include features such as marble sinks and hydro-massage shower stalls.

TownHouse Galleria
MAP M4 ▪ Via Silvio
Pellico 8 ▪ 02-3659-690
▪ http://galleria.town
househotels.com ▪ €€€
The exclusive location
within the lovely Galleria
Vittorio Emanuele II
arcade makes any stay
here a memorable one.
Rooms are equipped with
contemporary technology
and furnished with stylish
design elements. The
hotel also has a top floor
fitness suite offering
wellness treatments.

Milan's Smaller
Hotels and B&Bs

Hotel Due Giardini
MAP P1 ▪ Via Benedetto
Marcello 47 ▪ 02-2952-
1093 ▪ www.hotel
duegiardini.it ▪ €
Set in a pleasant location,
convenient for, but not too
close to, the station, and
with the shops in Corso
Buenos Aires just a short
walk away, this hotel
offers great value for
money. As its name sug-
gests, it really does have
two gardens, which are
perfect when you want a
break from Milan's gritty
urban cityscape.

Hotel Palladio
MAP P6 ▪ Via Palladio 8
▪ 02-5830-6900 ▪ www.
hotelpalladio.eu ▪ €
This is a typical 1920s
town house, in a quiet
residential street very near
the lively Porta Romana
area with its many bars,
shops and restaurants. It
offers excellent value, with
special rates from June to
August. Many rooms have
balconies and all have
satellite TV. No breakfast
is served but there's a
café a few minutes' walk
away which has warm

brioche (sweet croissants)
and creamy cappuccinos
for a couple of euros.

Hotel S. Biagio
MAP P1 ▪ Via Paganini 6
▪ 02-204-7443 ▪ www.
hotel-san-biagio-it.book.
direct ▪ €
Staying at this tiny hotel
on a residential street
off Corso Buenos Aires
is like moving in with
friends. The ten high-
ceilinged rooms are large
and comfortable, and all
have a private bathroom.
Rooms are equipped
with TV and free Wi-Fi.

Hotel Sempione
MAP M5 ▪ Via Finocchiaro
Aprile 11 ▪ 02-6570-323
▪ www.hotelsempione
milan.com ▪ €
This hotel, between the
train station and Piazza
del Duomo, is close to
the shopping and enter-
tainment hub of Corso
Buenos Aires. The airy
and simple rooms offer
every modern comfort.

San Francisco
MAP P1 ▪ Viale Lombardia
55 ▪ 02-236-1009 ▪ www.
hotel-sanfrancisco.it ▪ €
This small, family-run
hotel is only six metro
stops from the Duomo
and three from the main
train station. Rooms are
sparse but adequate and
there is a pretty garden
with pergola, lawn and
terrace where breakfast
is served in the summer.

Vecchia Milano
MAP L4 ▪ Via Borromei 4
▪ 02-875-042 ▪ www.
hotel vecchiamilano.it
▪ €
This hotel is at the high
end of inexpensive, but it's
worth it for the charming,
semi-rustic wooden

panelling, good-sized
rooms and location on
a quiet street west of
the Duomo. Some of the
rooms come with a third
bed that folds down from
the wall, which is great
for families on a budget.

Villa Magnolia
MAP J6 ▪ Via Ambrogio
Binda 32 ▪ 02-8130-200
▪ www.bbvillamagnolia.it
▪ €
This attractive early 1900s
villa is set in a residential
area close to the Navigli
district, just south of the
city centre, and offers
bed-and-breakfast
accommodation. It has
two double rooms and
one suite, sleeping three,
and there is satellite TV.

Antica Locanda
Leonardo
MAP J3 ▪ Corso Magneta
78 ▪ 02-4801-4197
▪ www.anticalocanda
leonardo.com ▪ €€
Situated in a residential
building just a couple of
minutes' walk from Santa
Maria delle Grazie, home
to Leonardo's *Last Supper*,
this family-run guest-
house with a charming
little garden offers a
peaceful retreat from
the bustle of the city.

Ariosto Hotel
MAP J2 ▪ Via Ariosto 22
▪ 02-481-7844 ▪ www.
hotelariosto.com ▪ €€
The Ariosto Hotel offers
luxurious amenities and
refined service without
a high price tag. Rooms
overlook the private
garden or open onto the
Liberty-style façades of
this residential street,
and all come with wood
furnishings and high-
speed Internet. Free bikes
are provided for guests.

Ariston
MAP K/L4 ■ Largo Carrobbio 2 ■ 02-7200-0556 ■ www. ariston hotel.com ■ €€

Offering a novel approach to Italian inn-keeping, the Ariston is an eco-hotel. The electrical devices here are engineered for low power consumption; the showers conserve water; the tap water and even the air are purified; the breakfast spread is organic. Naturally, the desk rents out Riciclo bicycles, which are ideal for exploring the city.

Capitol
MAP C5 ■ Via Cimarosa 6 ■ 02-438-591 ■ www.hotel capitolmilano.com ■ €€

This towering modern hotel boasts the latest in business technologies, as well as a fitness centre and rare on-site parking. Free Wi-Fi is available throughout the hotel, but guest rooms also include free fibre-optic broadband and flat-screen HD TV.

Doria Grand Hotel
MAP S2 ■ Viale Andrea Doria 22 ■ 02-6741-1411 ■ www.doriagrandhotel.it ■ €€

This is a large hotel with modern, comfortable rooms, four conference rooms, and secretarial services. It's ideal for a business trip but, as with many hotels in Milan, special discount rates are available on weekends.

Genius Hotel Downtown
MAP L3 ■ Via Porlezza 4 ■ 02-7209-4644 ■ www. hotelgenius.it ■ €€

This cosy modern hotel is on a quiet street beside the Castello. Rooms are compact but modern and clean, with bright, thick carpets, orthopaedic beds and largish baths.

Gran Duca di York
MAP L4 ■ Via Moneta 1a ■ 02-874-863 ■ www. ducadiyork.com ■ €€

In the 19th century this palazzo was used by the nearby cathedral to house visiting cardinals. Today, rooms have comfortable, modern furnishings, and some have terraces. The location in the historic centre is a real bonus.

Hotel Galileo
MAP N4 ■ Corso Europa 9 ■ 02-77-431 ■ galileo hotelmilan.com ■ €€

This modern four-star hotel in the heart of Milan is centrally located and within easy reach of the Duomo and the trendy shopping district. The 89 spacious rooms have free Wi-Fi.

London
MAP L3 ■ Via Rovello 3 ■ 02-7202-0166 ■ www. hotellondonmilano.com ■ €€

The most old-fashioned of three hotels on a block near the Castello offers smiling service, bright, large rooms with worn but solid furnishings, and 10 per cent off the next-door restaurant. Rooms get smaller as you go up each floor, so try to book one on a lower floor.

Maison Borella
MAP K6 ■ Alzaia Naviglio Grande 8■ 02 5810 9114 ■ www.hotelmaison borella.com ■ €€

Overlooking the canal and with an internal courtyard, this attractive hotel has simple rooms and offers a good base among the bars and restaurants of the Navigli district.

Marriott
MAP R2 ■ Via Washington 66 ■ 02-48-521 ■ www. marriott.com ■ €€

With 20 meeting rooms, a well-equipped business centre and a whole floor of Executive rooms, the Milan Marriott was built for the business traveller. Convenient for the Via Wagner and Piazza De Angeli shopping streets; if only it were nearer the centre for sightseeing when meetings are over.

Mediolanum
MAP P1 ■ Via Mauro Macchi 1 ■ 02-670-5312 ■ www.mediolanum hotel.com ■ €€

The austerity of this cement-grey hotel is relieved by the personal touch brought by family management. Facilities include a business centre with secretarial services, and there is valet parking.

Starhotel Anderson
MAP S2 ■ Piazza Luigi di Savoia 20 ■ 02-669-0141 ■ www.starhotels.com ■ €€

This design hotel offers sleek, modern decor. Expect beautiful fabrics, wooden panelling, large, comfortable beds and sumptuous marble bath-rooms. It is located next to Stazione Centrale and is just a short walk from Giardini Pubblici. The restaurant, Black, serves first-rate international and local dishes. Guests have access to meeting rooms as well as a fully equipped 24-hour fitness room. There is free Wi-Fi in all the guest rooms.

Tocq Hotel
MAP R2 ▪ Via A. De Tocqueville 7/D ▪ 02-62-071 ▪ www.tocq.it ▪ €€
Situated near the Corso Como and the Porta Nuova district, and close to the Garibaldi metro station, this hotel has well-equipped and modern rooms. Rooms have free Wi-Fi, satellite TV and minibars. Both Italian and American breakfasts are offered.

Una Hotel Century
MAP S2 ▪ Via F Filzi 25B ▪ 02-675-041 ▪ www.unahotels.it ▪ €€
Near the central station, north of Piazza della Repubblica, this property is made up entirely of sleek, modern business suites, each with a bedroom and separate living room/office. It's ideal for a short working visit.

Zurigo
MAP L5-M5 ▪ Corso Italia 11a ▪ 02-7202-2260 ▪ www.brerahotels.com ▪ €€
Although the entrance is on a busy street, just five minutes' walk from Piazza del Duomo, the compact but well-equipped rooms face the back of the hotel and are very quiet. Riciclo bicycles are available to guests free of charge.

3 Rooms
MAP L2 ▪ Corso Como 10, 20154 Milan ▪ 02 626163 ▪ www.3rooms-10corsocomo.com ▪ €€€
Part of the fashionable 10 Corso Como complex (see p70) each of three suites has its own independent entrance. The quirky and colourful decor features iconic design items.

Antica Locanda Solferino
MAP M1 ▪ Via Castelfidardo 2 ▪ 02-657-0129 ▪ www.antica locandasolferino.it ▪ €€€
Milan's most eccentric hotel is beloved by celebrities. What it lacks in amenities, it makes up for with its flower-fringed balconies, its homely, mismatched furnishings and breakfast in bed.

Hotel Lancaster
MAP J1 ▪ Via Abbondio Sangiorgio 16 ▪ 02-344-705 ▪ www.hotel lancaster.it ▪ €€€
A lovely Art Nouveau-style town house in a peaceful residential street right by Parco Sempione, this hotel is within easy reach of the centre of the city. A real find, it offers great prices, especially in June and July. Some rooms have terraces. Closed three weeks in August.

Hotel Tiziano
MAP R2 ▪ Via Tiziano 6 ▪ 02-469-9035 ▪ www.hoteltizianomilano.it ▪ €€€
Set within a 1930s palace designed by architect Piero Portaluppi, this hotel is situated in a pretty area, with rooms overlooking a large, tranquil park. It is also just a short walk to Fieramilano City. Rooms are warmly furnished and come with free Wi-Fi.

Santa Marta Suites
MAP L4 ▪ Via Santa Marta 4 ▪ 02 4537 3369 ▪ www.santamartasuites.com ▪ €€€
A timeless atmosphere is enhanced by historical architectural elements and antique furnishings in the beautifully designed rooms and suites on offer here. The top-floor terrace has views over the rooftops to the city's stunning cathedral.

Westin Palace
MAP N1 ▪ Piazza della Repubblica 20 ▪ 02-63-361 ▪ www.westin palacemilan.com ▪ €€€
The general decor of the historic Westin Palace is a genteel Empire style, but the "smart rooms" have lots of high-tech facilities, and the plush business centre offers on-staff translators and 13 well-equipped conference rooms. There is also a fully equipped gym.

Places to Stay in the Lakes and in Smaller Towns

Agnello d'Oro, Bergamo
MAP D3 ▪ Via Gombito 22 ▪ 035-249-883 ▪ www.agnellodoro.it ▪ €
Built in 1600, the "golden lamb" hotel has a mountain chalet look to it. The receptionists can be a bit brusque, but the rooms are cosy, if unimaginatively furnished. Book a room at the front, where small, flower-filled balconies provide views over the bustling main drag below.

Antico Chiostro, Como
MAP C3 ▪ Via Lambertenghi 4, 22100 Como, Lake Como ▪ 347 0632 137 ▪ www.antico chiostro.info ▪ €
At this comfortable and welcoming bed-and-breakfast in Como's attractive historic centre, the two suites have beautiful country-style decor, en-suite facilities and a small kitchen area.

Broletto, Mantua

MAP H6 ▪ Via Accademia
1 ▪ 0376-326-784 ▪ www.
hotelbroletto.com ▪ €

This is a small, family-run
hotel, housed in a 16th-
century palazzo with a
vaguely rustic contem-
porary decor. It is in a
lovely location, just a few
steps from Lake Inferiore.

Hotel Impero, Cremona

MAP E6 ▪ Piazza della
Pace 21 ▪ 0372-413-013
▪ www.hotelimpero.cr.it
▪ €

The 53 rooms of this hotel
are elegantly decorated,
blending period furniture
with modern facilities.
There is a smart wellness
area. Located in the town
centre, the Imperio offers
views over the cathedral
square and the town hall.

Le Rêve, Sirmione

MAP G4 ▪ Piazza Carducci
26 ▪ 349 8805 310
▪ www.lerevesirmione.it
▪ €

This friendly bed-and-
breakfast in the centre of
Sirmione has four rooms
decorated in a charming
smart country-style decor.
Some have a terrace
overlooking the piazza
and Lake Garda beyond.

La Veranda, Iseo

MAP F3 ▪ Largo Dante 5
▪ 335-635-2947
▪ bblaverandaiseo.
weebly.com ▪ €

This B&B has a spacious,
vine-covered terrace overlooking one of Iseo's
pretty piazzas, close to
the lake. Owner Flavio
enjoys sharing his local
knowledge and is alwasy
happy to take his guests
on a walk round the town
or out on a tour of the
Franciacorta vineyards.

Bellavista, Brunate

MAP C3 ▪ Piazza
Bonacossa 2 ▪ 031-221-
031 ▪ www.bella
vistabrunate.com ▪ €€

This Art Nouveau hotel
has stunning views over
Lake Como from most
rooms, as well as from
the restaurant and the
garden. Located close to
the funicular station at
Brunate it is easy to reach
from Como. The small
spa has a colour therapy
sauna and a Jacuzzi.

La Casa di Gabri, Clusane d'Iseo

MAP E4 ▪ Via
Risorgimento Trav.
Tredicesima 2 ▪ 349-291-
0479 ▪ www.lacasadi
gabri.com ▪ €€

This lovely B&B close to
Lake Iseo has appealing
fresh country-style decor,
a wide and shady veranda
and a large outdoor pool
and garden. Gabriella,
also owner and chef at
the nearby Trattoria del
Porto, provides a varied
and delicious breakfast.

Iseolago, Iseo

MAP E4 ▪ Via Colombera
2 ▪ 030-98-891 ▪ www.
iseolagohotel.it ▪ €€

The Iseolago is situated
near the Torbiere nature
reserve and mixes the
best of a resort hotel with
the class of a fine inn.
There is a fitness centre,
two pools, tennis courts,
and watersports at the
beach. It is in the suburbs,
so you will need a car.

Olivi, Sirmione

MAP G4 ▪ Via San Pietro
in Mavino 5 ▪ 030-990-
5365 ▪ www.hotelolivi.
com ▪ €€

Just a short stroll from
Sirmione's busy centre,
and on the shore of Lake
Garda, this smart hotel's
facilities include both
indoor and outdoor
thermal-heated pools and
an open-air swimming
pool in summer. Some
rooms have lake views.

L'Albereta, Erbusco

MAP E4 ▪ Via Vittorio
Emanuele 23 ▪ 030-7760
550 ▪ www.albereta.it
▪ €€€

This gorgeous country-
house hotel is owned by
the prestigious Bellavista
winery and has lovely
views over Lake Iseo.
There are two restau-
rants, a spa and lovely
grounds. Some rooms
have frescoes and are
furnished with antiques.

Sheraton Lake Como, Cernobbio

MAP C3 ▪ Via per
Cernobbio 41A ▪ 031-
5161 ▪ sheratonlake
como.com ▪ €€€

A contemporary hotel
with comfortable and
stylish interiors, an outdoor pool and pizzeria. It's
a five-minute walk from
the Tavernola ferry stop
so makes an ideal base,
for exploring Lake Como.

Villa Crespi, Lake Orta

MAP A3 ▪ Via Fava, 18
▪ 0322-911-902 ▪ www.
villacrespi.it ▪ Closed
Jan–Feb ▪ €€€

Villa Crespi is a fantastical
1879 Moorish-style villa,
complete with minaret,
set against a backdrop
of mountains. Suites and
rooms are sumptuous,
with mosaic or parquet
flooring, carved wooden
furnishings, silk brocaded
walls, and bed canopies.
The two-Michelin-starred
restaurant offers three
tasting menus (see p133).

Villa della Torre, Fumane

MAP H4 ▪ Via della Torre 25 ▪ 045-683-2070 ▪ www.villadellatorre.it ▪ €€€

Surrounded by vineyards, this Renaissance villa is owned by the Allegrini wine-making dynasty, The grounds and interior of the villa, particularly the statuesque monster fireplaces downstairs, are simply breathtaking.

Self-Catering and Campsites

Campeggio Città di Milano

MAP Q2 ▪ Via G Airaghi 61 ▪ 02-4820-7017 ▪ www.campingmilano.it ▪ €

Milan's only campsite is by the SS22 (take bus 72 from the De Angeli Metro stop) near the San Siro stadium. It has a restaurant and some tents are suspended between the trees.

Campeggio Garda Giulia, Limone

MAP G3 ▪ Via 4 Novembre 10 ▪ 0365-954-550 ▪ www.campinglagodigarda.it ▪ Closed Nov–Mar ▪ €

Just outside Limone, on its own private Garda beach, this site offers windsurfing and sailing, two pools, a fish restaurant, wood-oven pizzeria, beach grill and shop.

Camping Conca d'Oro, Feriolo di Baveno

MAP A2 ▪ Via 42 Martiri 26 ▪ 0323-281-16 ▪ www.concadoro.it ▪ Closed Oct–Mar ▪ €

This verdant campsite is located outside Baveno, on Lake Maggiore in the Fondo Toce nature reserve. Amenities here include a restaurant and a mini-market, bikes and kayaks, plus a sandy beach.

Camping del Sole, Lake Iseo

MAP E4 ▪ Via per Rovato 26 ▪ 030-980-288 ▪ www.campingdelsole.it ▪ Closed Oct–Mar ▪ €

This large camping site offers plenty of greenery right on the lake (book ahead for the coveted few lakeside sites). Facilities include a restaurant, a market and a laundry, as well as bike hire, two pools and tennis and basketball courts.

Camping Isolino, Verbania

MAP A2 ▪ Via per Feriolo 25 ▪ 0323-496-414 ▪ www.campingisolino.com ▪ Closed Oct–Mar ▪ €

This oasis of tranquillity sits on the promontory of a Lake Maggiore nature reserve along a private sandy beach. It's one of the best equipped camp-sites in the entire region, with a market, pizzeria, restaurant, swimming pool, mountain-bike excursions, windsurfing and entertainment.

Camping Monte Brione, Riva del Garda

MAP H3 ▪ Via Brione 32 ▪ 0464-520-885 ▪ www.campingbrione.com ▪ Closed Oct–Mar ▪ €

Set in greenery near a beach on Lake Garda, this four-star camping and caravan site has minigolf, a swimming pool and table tennis. Small tents can be pitched on terraces of ancient olive trees.

Camping Villaggio Gefara, Domaso

MAP C2 ▪ Via Case Sparse 230 ▪ 0344-96-163 ▪ www.campinggefara.it ▪ Closed 6 Oct–20 Mar ▪ €

This small campsite sits right on the beach on Lake Como, and has a bar and laundry room. There are plenty of shops and watersports nearby.

Residence Aramis Milano, Milan

MAP J6 ▪ Via Mortara 2 ▪ 340-084-8590 ▪ www.residencearamismilano.it ▪ €€

Overlooking a canal in the lively Navigli district, this "aparthotel" has accom modation ranging from rooms to fully equipped apartments sleeping six. All clean and spacious, and come with free Wi-Fi.

Serego Alighieri, Sant'Ambrogio di Valpolicella

MAP H4 ▪ Via Stazione Vecchia, Gargagnago ▪ 045-770-3622 ▪ seregoalighieri.it ▪ €€

Set in part of the historic wine estate run by the descendants of medieval poet Dante, these lovely apartments have beamed ceilings, wooden floors and their own kitchen. Breakfast is served in the main dining area.

Milanosuites, Milan

MAP L3 ▪ Via San Tomaso 6 ▪ 02-8051-023 ▪ www.milanosuites.it ▪ €€€

A sister operation of, and located next to, the Antica Locanda dei Mercanti (see p144), these five elegant suites have one or two bedrooms with en-suite bathroom and living room. There are special rates for weekly rentals.

Index

Acknowledgments

Author

Reid Bramblett is a travel writer who has authored guides to Italy, Europe and New York, as well as DK's *Top 10 Travel Guide to Tuscany*.

Additional contributor
Sarah Lane

Publishing Director Georgina Dee

Publisher Vivien Antwi

Design Director Phil Ormerod

Editorial Ankita Awasthi Tröger, Rachel Fox, Fay Franklin, Maresa Manera, Alison McGill Sally Schafer, Beverly Smart, Rachel Thompson

Cover Design Richard Czapnik

Design Marisa Renzullo, Bharti Karakoti

Picture Research Susie Peachey, Ellen Root, Lucy Sienkowska

Cartography James Anderson, Deshpal Dabas, Casper Morris, Jane Voss

DTP Jason Little

Production Jude Crozier

Factchecker Cristina Dainotto

Proofreader Leena Lane

Indexer Helen Peters

Commissioned Photography Helena Smith

First edition created by BLUE ISLAND PUBLISHING, London

Picture Credits

The publisher would like to thank the following for their kind permission to reproduce their photographs:
(**Key:** a-above; b-below/bottom; c-centre; f-far; l-left; r-right; t-top)

10 Corso Como: 70t.

123RF.com: Giorgio Bizzotto 112tl; Claudiodivizia 11cra, 28bl, 28–9, 91br; elesi 106tl; jakobradlgruber 34–5; Vladimir Korostyshevskiy 58clb.

4Corners: Günter Gräfenhain 108br, 113tr; SIME / Luca Da Ros 46bl, 125b.

Abbazia di Chiaravalle: Altin Manaf 58tr.

Aimo e Nadia: Ph F. Bolis_artworks P.Ferrari 66b.

Alamy Stock Photo: AEP 43cr; age fotostock / Mats Silvan 82t; Bailey-Cooper Photography 10b, 22–3; Mark Daffey 6cla; dpa picture alliance 77cl; Adam Eastland 69cl; Elizabeth Whiting & Associates / ewastock objects 86c; Godong 16cra; hemis.fr / Ludovic Maisant 88t; John Warburton-Lee Photography / Christian Kober 7tr; Joana Kruse 74cla; LOOK Die Bildagentur der Fotografen GmbH / Ingolf Pompe 6b, 30cla; MARKA / Giovanni Mereghetti 68tl; Realy Easy Star / Giuseppe Masci 74b; Patti

McConville 72cl; Jawad Qasrawi 128cl; Reda &Co Srl 10clb, 67tl, / Michele Bella 89bl, / Eddy Buttarelli 4cl; Grant Rooney 124cl; SFM MILAN (Italy) 29crb, 87br; Hugh Threlfall 85c; tofino 1; Ivan Vdovin 11tc, 99tl; Michael Ventura 73cl; Federica Violin 2tl, 8–9.

Archivio Museo Nazionale della Scienza e della Tecnologia Leonardo da Vinci: Lorenza Daverio 99br; Alessandro Grassani 60bl; Lorenza Laverio 44cl.

AWL Images: Walter Bibikow 4clb, 107cra; Marco Bottigelli 3tr, 132bl, 134–5; ClickAlps 118br, 130tl; Hemis 4t; Francesco Iacobelli 3tl, 78–9; Stefano Politi Markovina 109cl.

Cantina Piemontese: 103b.

Cavallie Nastri: 102tl.

Citta del Sole: 87c.

Trattoria Da Abele: 97cla.

Don Lisander: 89cra.

Dreamstime.com: Aladin66 34cl; Andersastphoto 64c, 76br; Andreadonetti 64tl; Leonid Andronov 4crb; Jennifer Barrow 14–5; Bennymarty 40tl; Roberto Binetti 11cr, 26–7, 100t; Eva Bocek 110b; Sergej Borzov 32–3; Armin Burkhardt 69tr; Byggarn79 92tr; Cathyr1 31tl, 117b; Claudiodivizia 20bl, 82br; Claudio Giovanni Colombo 26br, 48cr, 91tl, 113br; Conde 41crb; Piero Cruciatti 72t; Olga Demchishina 107b; Elitravo 129t; Ellesi 30–1; Endomass77 28cl; Ermess 57tr; Fashionstock.com / Antonoparin 76c; Fabio Formaggio 14l; Freesurf69 7br; Viktor Gladkov 50tl; GoneWithTheWind 48br; Yevgenia Gorbulsky 126cr; Jorg Hackemann 81t; Wang Haijie 53br; Neil Harrison 115cl; Ilongplay 11bl; Ixuskmitl 40b, 51tr; Vladislav Jirousek 56tr; Jojjik 59b, 130–1; Alexandra King 75cla; Vladimir Korostyshevskiy 98tl; Kuvona 65clb; Elisa Locci 43tl; Olga Lupol 4cla; Oleksandr Lysenko 70bl; Roberto Maggioni 47cra; Maigi 4cra; Ranko Maras 15cr; Nadia Mikushova 76tl; Morseicinque 11crb, 116tr; Andrey Omelyanchuk 42b; Franco Ricci 81br; Rigamondis 121b; Arseniy Rogov 49b; Valeria Sangiovanni 85tl; Santanor 10c; Marco Saracco 48tr, 123bl; Juergen Schonnop 46t; Marco Scisetti 114b; Jozef Sedmak 94br; Serghei Starus 122t; Thanate191 61clb; Thejipen 33bl; Toldiu74 60t; Antonio Truzzi 26cla; Raluca Tudor 75tr; Tupungato 93cl; Umbertoleporini 51l; Gian Marco Valente 122c; Valentino Visentini 71tr; Bruce Whittingham 15bc; Xantana 4b.

Festa dell'Uva e del vino Bardolino: 77tr.

By concession of Fondazione Accademia Carrara, Bergamo: Tiffany Pesenti 33crb; Gianfranco Rota 32cla.

Frette: 86t.

Getty Images: Sunset Boulevard 53cl; Morena

Brengola 102cr; Vittorio Zunino Celotto 55cla; De Agostini 38tl, / Biblioteca Ambrosiana 39tr; DEA 24cla, / G. Cigolini 19bl, 21tl, 21bl, 80l, / G. Nimatallah 38b, / M. Carrieri 19cra, 90tl, / Veneranda Biblioteca Ambrosiana 24crb; Krzysztof Dydynski 27br; Heritage Images 25br, 83cl, / Fine Art Images 54t; Sergione Infuso 62tl, 63crb; Maremagnum 35cl, 131cl; Roberto Mettifogo 121cr; Mondadori Portfolio 20–1, / Electa / Sergio Anelli 20cla, / Fotografo / Agenzia 100c, / Reporters Associati & Archivi / Angelo Novi 52br, / Sergio Anelli 45c; Olaf Protze 30crb; Mats Silvan 2tr, 36–7; Manuel Sulzer 116clb; Karwai Tang 73tr; UIG / AGF / Nardi Alberto 126tl, La Monaca Davide 29tl, / Universal History Archive Portrait of Alessandro Manzoni by Francesco Hayez 52cl.

Hotel Verbano: 111c.

iStockphoto.com: AndreasWeber 108t; bonottomario 129br; rudisill 65tl; titoslack 101cla; Flavio Vallenari 57cl, 104–5.

Joia: A. Mauri 97cb.

Lo Scalo: 111tr.

Locanda dell'Isola Comacina: 119cra.

Museo Poldi Pezzoli, Milan: 45tl.

Museo Teatrale alla Scala: 50b, 62b, 84b.

Pinacoteca di Brera: 16cl, 17tl, 17crb, 17bl, 18tl, 18cr, 19tl, 92bl.

Post-Design: Simone Bacchetti 95t.

Rex Shutterstock: Silver Films / Sotiledip / Nepi 53tl; UIG / Mondadori Electa Electa 10cla, 12–3, 13cr, 13tl, 13bl.

Ricci: 96b.

Ristorante Vecchia Malcesine: 127cr.

Robert Harding Picture Library: Riccardo Sala 35tl; Andreas Strauss 114tl.

Photo Scala, Florence: DeAgostini Picture Library / Veneranda Biblioteca Ambrosiana 11tl, 25tl, 44br, 54bl; White Images 39cl.

SuperStock: age fotostock / Yoko Aziz 118ca; Cubo Images 55br; imageBROKER / imageb / gourmet-vision 67br; Marka 64br, 65br, / Jader Alto 61tr; Prisma 124tr.

Villa Crespi: 133cla.

Villa Fiordaliso: Nicolo' Brunelli 66cla.

Zucca (Caffè Miani): 68br.

Cover

Front and spine – **Alamy Stock Photo:** LOOK Die Bildagentur der Fotografen GmbH. Back – **Dreamstime.com:** lxuskmitl.

Pull out map cover

Alamy Stock Photo: LOOK Die Bildagentur der Fotografen GmbH.

All other images are: © Dorling Kindersley. For further information see www.dkimages.com.

As a guide to abbreviations in visitor information blocks: **Adm** = admission charge; **DA** = disabled access.

Penguin
Random
House

Printed and bound in China

First published in Great Britain in 2003 by Dorling Kindersley Limited 80 Strand, London WC2R 0RL

Copyright 2003, 2018 © Dorling Kindersley Limited

A Penguin Random House Company

18 19 20 21 10 9 8 7 6 5 4 3 2 1

Reprinted with revisions 2005, 2007, 2009, 2011, 2013, 2015, 2018

A CIP catalogue record is available from the British Library.

ISBN 978 0 2412 9633 2

MIX
Paper from responsible sources
FSC™ C018179

SPECIAL EDITIONS OF DK TRAVEL GUIDES

DK Travel Guides can be purchased in bulk quantities at discounted prices for use in promotions or as premiums. We are also able to offer special editions and personalized jackets, corporate imprints, and excerpts from all of our books, tailored specifically to meet your own needs.

To find out more, please contact:

in the US
specialsales@dk.com

in the UK
travelguides@uk.dk.com

in Canada
specialmarkets@dk.com

in Australia
penguincorporatesales@ penguinrandomhouse.com.au

Phrase Book

In an Emergency

Help!	Aiuto!	eye-yoo-toh
Stop!	Ferma!	fair-mah
Call a doctor.	Chiama un medico.	kee-ah-mah oon meh-dee-koh
Call an ambulance.	Chiama un' ambulanza.	kee-ah-mah oon am-boo-lan-tsa
Call the police.	Chiama la polizia.	kee-ah-mah lah pol-ee-tsee-ah
Call the fire brigade.	Chiama i pompieri.	kee-ah-mah ee pom-pee-air-ee

Communication Essentials

Yes/No	Sì/No	see/noh
Please	Per favore	pair fah-vor-eh
Thank you	Grazie	grah-tsee-eh
Excuse me	Mi scusi	mee skoo-zee
Hello	Buon giorno	bwon jor-noh
Goodbye	Arrivederci	ah-ree-veh-dair-chee
Good evening	Buona sera	bwon-ah sair-ah
What?	Quale?	kwah-leh?
When?	Quando?	kwan-doh?
Why?	Perché?	pair-keh?
Where?	Dove?	doh-veh?

Useful Phrases

How are you?	Come sta?	koh-meh stah?
Very well, thank you.	Molto bene, grazie.	moll-toh beh-neh grah-tsee-eh
Pleased to meet you.	Piacere di conoscerla.	pee-ah-chair-eh dee-coh-noh-shair-lah
That's fine.	Va bene.	va beh-neh
Where is/are …?	Dov'è/ Dove sono …?	dov-eh/doveh soh-noh…?
How do I get to …?	Come faccio per arrivare a …?	koh-meh fah-choh pair arri-var-eh ah…?
Do you speak English?	Parla inglese?	par-lah een-gleh-zeh?
I don't understand.	Non capisco.	non ka-pee-skoh
I'm sorry.	Mi dispiace.	mee dee-spee-ah-cheh

Shopping

How much does this cost?	Quant'è, per favore?	kwan-the pair fah-vor-eh?
I would like …	Vorrei …	vor-ray
Do you have …?	Avete …?	ah-veh-teh…?
Do you take credit cards?	Accettate carte di credito?	ah-chet-tah-the kar-teh dee creh-dee-toh?
What time do you open/close?	A che ora apre/ chiude?	ah keh or-ah ah-preh/ kee-oo-deh?
this one	questo	kweh-stoh
that one	quello	kwell-oh
expensive	caro	kar-oh
cheap	a buon prezzo	ah bwon pret-soh
size, clothes	la taglia	lah tah-lee-ah
size, shoes	il numero	eel noo-mair-oh
white	bianco	bee-ang-koh
black	nero	neh-roh
red	rosso	ross-oh
yellow	giallo	jal-loh
green	verde	vair-deh
blue	blu	bloo

Types of Shop

bakery	il forno /il panificio	eel forn-oh /il /eel pan-ee-fee-choh
bank	la banca	lah bang-kah
bookshop	la libreria	lah lee-breh-ree-ah
cake shop	la pasticceria	lah pas-tee-chair-ee-ah
chemist	la farmacia	lah far-mah-chee-ah
delicatessen	la salumeria	lah sah-loo-meh-ree-ah
department store	il grande magazzino	eel gran-deh mag-gad-zee-noh
grocery	alimentari	ah-lee-men-tah-ree
hairdresser	il parrucchiere	eel par-oo-kee-air-eh
ice cream parlour	la gelateria	lah jel-lah-tair-ree-ah
market	il mercato	eel mair-kah-toh
newsstand	l'edicola	leh-dee-koh-lah
post office	l'ufficio postale	loo-fee-choh pos-tah-leh
supermarket	il supermercato	eel su-pair-mair-kah-toh
tobacconist	il tabaccaio	eel tah-bak-eye-oh
travel agency	l'agenzia di viaggi	lah-jen-tsee-ah dee vee-ad-jee

Sightseeing

art gallery	la pinacoteca	lah peena-koh-teh-kah
bus stop	la fermata dell'autobus	lah fair-mah-tah dell ow-toh-booss
church	la chiesa/ la basilica	lah kee-eh-zah/ lah bah-seel-i-kah
closed for holidays	chiuso per le ferie	kee-oo-zoh pair leh fair-ee-eh
garden	il giardino	eel jar-dee-no
museum	il museo	eel moo-zeh-oh
railway station	la stazione	lah stah-tsee-oh-neh
tourist information	l'ufficio di turismo	loo-fee-choh dee too-ree-smoh

Staying in a Hotel

Do you have any vacant rooms?	Avete camere libere?	ah-veh-teh kah-mair-eh lee-bair-eh?
double room	una camera doppia	oona kah-mair-ah doh-pee-ah
with double bed	con letto matrimoniale	kon let-toh mah-tree-moh-nee-ah-leh
twin room	una camera con due letti	oona kah-mair-ah kon doo-eh let-tee
single room	una camera singola	oona kah-mair ah sing-goh-la
room with a bath, shower	una camera con bagno, con doccia	oona kah-mair ah kon ban-yoh, kon dot-cha
I have a reservation.	Ho fatto una prenotazione.	oh fat-toh oona preh-noh-tsee-oh-n

Eating Out

Have you got a table for ...?	**Avete un tavolo per ...?**	ah-veh-teh oon tah-voh-lah pair ...?
I'd like to reserve a table	**Vorrei riservare un tavolo.**	vor-ray ree-sair-vah-reh oon tah-voh-lah
breakfast	**colazione**	koh-lah-tsee-oh-neh
lunch	**pranzo**	pran-tsoh
dinner	**cena**	cheh-nah
The bill, please.	**Il conto, per favore.**	eel kon-toh pair fah-vor-eh
waitress	**cameriera**	kah-mair-ee-air-ah
waiter	**cameriere**	kah-mair-ee-aireh
fixed price menu	**il menù a prezzo fisso**	eel meh-noo ah pret-soh fee-soh
dish of the day	**piatto del giorno**	pee-ah-toh dell jor-no
starter	**antipasto**	an-tee-pass-toh
first course	**il primo**	eel pree-moh
main course	**il secondo**	eel seh-kon-doh
vegetables	**contorni**	eel kon-tor-noh
dessert	**il dolce**	eel doll-cheh
cover charge	**il coperto**	eel koh-pair-toh
wine list	**la lista dei vini**	lah lee-stah day vee-nee
glass	**il bicchiere**	eel bee-kee-air-eh
bottle	**la bottiglia**	lah bot-teel-yah
knife	**il coltello**	eel kol-tell-oh
fork	**la forchetta**	lah for-ket-tah
spoon	**il cucchiaio**	eel koo-kee-eye-oh

Menu Decoder

l'acqua minerale	lah-kwah mee-nair-ah-leh	mineral water
gassata/ naturale	gah-zah-tah/ nah-too-rah-leh	fizzy/still
agnello	ah-niell-oh	lamb
aglio	al-ee-oh	garlic
al forno	al for-noh	baked
alla griglia	ah-lah greel-yah	grilled
arrosto	ar-ross-toh	roast
la birra	lah beer-rah	beer
la bistecca	lah bee-stek-kah	steak
il burro	eel boor-oh	butter
il caffè	eel kah-feh	coffee
la carne	la kar-neh	meat
carne di maiale	kar-neh dee mah-yah-leh	pork
la cipolla	la chip-oh-lah	onion
fagioli	ee fah-joh-lee	beans
formaggio	eel for-mad-joh	cheese
...gole	leh frah-goh-leh	strawberries
...h misto	eel free-toh mees-toh	mixed fried dish
	la froot-tah	fruit
...are	froo-tee dee mah-reh	seafood
	ee foon-ghee	mushrooms
	ee gam-bair-ee	prawns
	eel jel-lah-toh	ice cream
	...een-sah-lah-tah	salad
	...l laht-teh	milk
	...-oh	boiled
	...nan-tsoh	beef
	...-oh	oil
	...-neh	bread
	...ah-teh	potatoes
le patatine fritte	leh pah-tah-teen-eh free-teh	chips
il pepe	eel peh-peh	pepper
il pesce	eel pesh-eh	fish
il pollo	eel poll-oh	chicken
il pomodoro	eel poh-moh-dor-oh	tomato
il prosciutto cotto/crudo	eel pro-shoo-toh kot-toh/kroo-doh	ham cooked/cured
il riso	eel ree-zoh	rice
il sale	eel sah-leh	salt
la salsiccia	lah sal-see-chah	sausage
succo d'arancia/ di limone	soo-koh dah-ran-chah/ dee lee-moh-neh	orange/lemon juice
il tè	eel teh	tea
la torta	lah tor-tah	cake/tart
l'uovo	loo-oh-voh	egg
vino bianco	vee-noh bee-ang-koh	white wine
vino rosso	vee-noh ross-oh	red wine
il vitello	eel vee-tell-oh	veal
le vongole	leh von-goh-leh	clams
lo zucchero	loh zoo-kair-oh	sugar
la zuppa	lah tsoo-pah	soup

Numbers

1	**uno**	oo-noh
2	**due**	doo-eh
3	**tre**	treh
4	**quattro**	kwat-roh
5	**cinque**	ching-kweh
6	**sei**	say-ee
7	**sette**	set-teh
8	**otto**	ot-toh
9	**nove**	noh-veh
10	**dieci**	dee-eh-chee
11	**undici**	oon-dee-chee
12	**dodici**	doh-dee-chee
13	**tredici**	tray-dee-chee
14	**quattordici**	kwat-tor-dee-chee
15	**quindici**	kwin-dee-chee
16	**sedici**	say-dee-chee
17	**diciassette**	dee-chah-set-the
18	**diciotto**	dee-chot-toh
19	**diciannove**	dee-chah-noh-veh
20	**venti**	ven-tee
30	**trenta**	tren-tah
40	**quaranta**	kwah-ran-tah
50	**cinquanta**	ching-kwan-tah
60	**sessanta**	sess-an-tah
70	**settanta**	set-tan-tah
80	**ottanta**	ot-tan-tah
90	**novanta**	noh-van-tah
100	**cento**	chen-toh
1,000	**mille**	mee-leh
2,000	**duemila**	doo-eh mee-lah
1,000,000	**un milione**	oon meel-yoh-neh

Time

one minute	**un minuto**	oon mee-noo-toh
one hour	**un'ora**	oon or-ah
a day	**un giorno**	oon jor-noh
Monday	**lunedì**	loo-neh-dee
Tuesday	**martedì**	mar-teh-dee
Wednesday	**mercoledì**	mair-koh-leh-dee
Thursday	**giovedì**	joh-veh-dee
Friday	**venerdì**	ven-air-dee
Saturday	**sabato**	sah-bah-toh
Sunday	**domenica**	doh-meh-nee-kah